Luther
Servant of God

Corbis

Student Book

Victor Paulos

CONCORDIA PUBLISHING HOUSE • SAINT LOUIS

Second edition
Copyright © 1966, 2003 by Concordia Publishing House,
3558 S. Jefferson Ave., St. Louis MO 63118-3968
1-800-325-3040 • www.cph.org

Edited by Clarence Berndt

Scripture quotations taken from the HOLY BIBLE, NEW INTERNATIONAL VERSION®. NIV®. Copyright 1973, 1978, 1984 by International Bible Society. Used by permission of Zondervan Publishing House. All rights reserved.

Quotations from the Lutheran Confessions are reprinted by permission from *The Book of Concord: The Confessions of the Evangelical Lutheran Church,* edited by Robert Kolb and Timothy J. Wengert, copyright © 2000 Augsburg Fortress, Minneapolis.

Some Luther quotations are from *What Luther Says,* compiled by Ewald M. Plass, copyright © 1959 Concordia Publishing House.

Photo Credits:

    Corbis: Title page, pp. 6, 10, 14, 15, 24, 26, 36, 39 (left), 44, 45, 56, 57, 61, 62, 63, 64, 73 (right), 74, 79, 84, 94

    Inside Missouri (February 2003), LCMS Missouri District: p. 5

    Luther and His Times (CPH): pp. 41, 51, 68, 73 (left), 77, 91

    Opera *Luther* and Kari Tikka: p. 31

    Picture-Alliance: pp. 11, 29, 35

    Pitts Theology Library Digital Image Archive: p. 34

This publication may be available in braille, in large print, or on cassette tape for the visually impaired. Please allow 8 to 12 weeks for delivery. Write to Lutheran Blind Mission, 7550 Watson Rd., St. Louis, MO 63119-4409; call toll-free 1-888-215-2455; or visit the Web site: www.blindmission.org.

Manufactured in the United States of America

    3 4 5 6 7 8 9 10   18 17 16 15 14 13 12

Contents

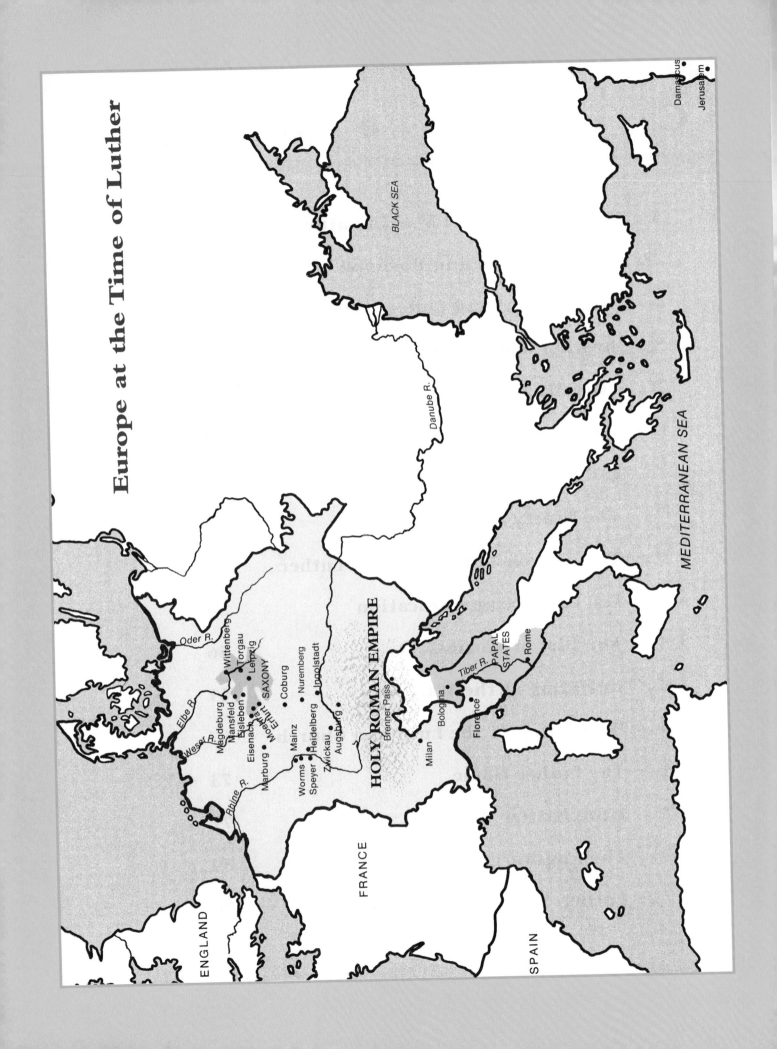

Europe at the Time of Luther

1 Why Study about Martin Luther?

Are you a Christian? Christians are people who trust in Jesus Christ as Savior and Lord. There are hundreds of millions of Christians in the world. Not all of them believe exactly the same things about Jesus or the teachings of the Bible. Roman Catholic Christians, Methodist Christians, and Baptist Christians have different teachings and practices, but all are followers of the same Lord and Master.

Some Christians are called Lutherans because they believe that what Martin Luther taught from the Bible about Jesus best explains the way to eternal life. In the Bible Luther discovered that a person is saved by grace, through faith in God's Son (Ephesians 2:8). Eternal life is a free gift of God to those who trust in Christ as their Savior from sin and death.

As you study the life of Luther, you will see how God can use sinful people to do His work on earth. Martin Luther, though sinful, was a special servant of God, as were the prophets and apostles of Bible times. Through the prophets and apostles God gave His people the message of life and forgiveness; through Luther He restored this message to its central place in the life of the church and emphasized for each person that the message of the Gospel is supremely important for his or her own life and salvation.

For the Christian, any study of Luther is done to grow in faith. People grow in faith primarily when they hear the Gospel spoken and when they receive the Sacraments. People may also grow in faith when they come into contact with great Christians who live and share God's Word with others. The Gospel can be seen at work in the lives of these heroes of faith. A study of Martin Luther's spiritual struggle

Principal David Buchholz instructs students about Luther at Holy Cross Lutheran Church, Kansas City, Mo.

LCMS Missouri District

5

Luther expressed the feelings of many medieval Christians toward Jesus when he wrote, "I was often frightened by the name of Christ, and when I looked upon Him and the cross, He seemed to me like a flash of lightning." He prayed to Mary to ask for mercy from Jesus.

and his life helps people see the glory of God's grace and gives His direction for their life's vocation.

The Times of Martin Luther

When Christopher Columbus sailed on his first voyage to America, Luther was just nine years old. He was born on November 10, 1483, or nearly 15 centuries after Jesus' birth in Bethlehem.

The teachings of Jesus had been spread far and wide by His first disciples. Other faithful preachers and teachers carried the Gospel to many lands, so that within a few hundred years after Jesus ascended into heaven, most people in Europe, northern Africa, and the Middle East were Christians.

The Christian church did not stay united. In the year 1054 the Christian church split into two large parts: the

Eastern, or Greek Orthodox Church; and the Western, or Roman Catholic Church. These two churches are still separate today. Smaller groups of Christians broke away from each of these two main bodies from time to time because they developed different beliefs or ways of worship. Over the years the gulf widened between the two churches, and many questionable practices developed within them. By Luther's time some of Christ's teachings were no longer being followed. The Mass had lost much of the spiritual emphasis of the Lord's Supper. People believed that in the celebration of the Mass Jesus was sacrificed again and that the bread and wine were completely changed into Christ's body and blood. The people received only the bread, and the priest drank the wine.

Christians were led to think of Jesus as being an angry Judge rather than a loving Savior. They were told to pray to His mother, Mary, to ask Him to be merciful and forgiving. Other saints, rather than God, were called on for special help.

Other False Teachings and Customs

The church taught that, even though sins were forgiven, it was necessary for people to make some type of payment to have their sins removed. For example, people were told to say the rosary many times to make up for doing a wrong. (To say the rosary refers to the practice of praying to Mary and saying the Lord's Prayer while meditating on various mysteries related to Christ. The prayers are counted by means of prayer beads that may also be referred to as a rosary.)

Since no one, not even the pope, could hope to repay God for all the sins committed during this life, people were taught that after they died they would have to suffer in purgatory for their sins before they could enter heaven (*purgatory* refers to a place where people are made clean). They were also taught that friends or relatives could get them out of purgatory earlier by saying prayers and making offerings to the church. In addition, people were taught that the more good works one could do in this life, the sooner he or she might go from purgatory to heaven. For this reason people made pilgrimages, or trips, to holy places such as those in Jerusalem and other parts of the Holy Land. Many people traveled to shrines, where relics of saints, such as clothing,

bones, hair, or similar objects, were kept. They believed that seeing, touching, and praying before these relics were good works.

People at Luther's time lived in fear of purgatory and hell. Never in their life could they be peaceful and happy. They believed that after death they would have to spend many years suffering before they could hope to go to heaven. The family and friends of a dead person had priests say masses in church to shorten the dead person's stay in purgatory. Sometimes people left much money to the church so that masses could be said for them after they died.

Into a world of such fear and false teaching Martin Luther was born. In this study we will go back to the time Luther lived, from 1483 to 1546. During these years God helped His servant carry out the great work of reforming the church and preserving for all of us today the Gospel message of salvation through Jesus.

Review Questions and Study Projects

1. Read each sentence carefully. If the sentence is true, circle the T. If it is false, circle the F.

T   F   a. All Christians worship together because they believe in the same God.

T   F   b. Lutherans are those who follow the teachings of Martin Luther.

T   F   c. Luther was a young boy when America was discovered.

T   F   d. The Christian religion did not spread outside the Holy Land until Luther's time.

T   F   e. Until Luther split it, the Christian church had always been one great, united body.

T   F   f. At Luther's time Jesus was looked upon as a stern, angry Judge.

T   F   g. The church taught that good works made up for sins.

T   F   h. People believed that purgatory was a place of punishment for unbelievers.

T   F   i. Before the time of Luther, religion was built more on fear than on hope.

2. What is the central teaching of the Lutheran church?

_____

_____

_____

_____

3. Study Ephesians 2:8–9 and write what you would say to someone who believes that good works save.

_____

_____

_____

_____

4. How do Luke 16:22–23 and Luke 23:43 show there is no purgatory?

_____

_____

_____

_____

5. Martin Luther was a faithful servant of God. Describe several ways in which you can serve God faithfully.

_____

_____

_____

_____

6. Write several reasons why the study of Martin Luther and his work is valuable.

_____

_____

_____

_____

_____

7. Look in a history book and find out what was happening in other countries during Luther's lifetime. In your notebook make a chart, or time line, placing some of these events on one side and events from Luther's life on the other side.

8. Define these words:

reformation _____

purgatory _____

orthodox _____

pilgrimage _____

Mass _____

relic _____

9. In Luther's time people made pilgrimages to places of religious significance. Design a travel folder for a "pilgrimage" of your own to one of the places listed below. Answer these questions as you describe your pilgrimage: How is the purpose of a pilgrimage today different from the purpose for which people made pilgrimages in Luther's day? What happened or happens at this place that is of religious significance? Does this place present its message well? What can you do here that will help you grow spiritually?

Jerusalem

Bethlehem

Wittenberg, Germany

Augsburg, Germany

Chartres Cathedral, France

National Cathedral, Washington, D.C.

Canterbury Cathedral, England

The Vatican, Rome, Italy

For it is by grace you have been saved, through faith—and this not from yourselves, it is the gift of God—not by works, so that no one can boast (Ephesians 2:8–9).

My Prayer

Thank You, loving Father in heaven, for sending servants such as Martin Luther to spread Your Word. Help me love and honor my pastors, teachers, and all those who serve You in their work. Keep me in the true faith through Your Holy Spirit. For Jesus' sake I ask this. Amen.

2 Luther's Birth and Boyhood

November 10, 1483, was a cold day in Eisleben, Germany. Yet in the home of Hans and Margaret Luther there was warmth and happiness. God had given them a son.

When the baby was only a day old, Hans took him to the Church of St. Peter. He wanted his son to be baptized and to become God's child. Since November 11 was the day in the church year set aside to honor St. Martin of Tours, Hans and Margaret named their son Martin.

Hans Luder, as his name was pronounced then, was an ambitious man who wanted to improve the financial position of his family. Six months after Martin was born the family moved to Mansfeld, about 10 miles away. Hans took a job as a copper miner. He worked hard and spent carefully. Within seven years he had started his own mining business. He was elected to be a member of Mansfeld's city council. Margaret Luther helped save money by gathering firewood in the forest, as did many of the women of the day.

God blessed Hans and Margaret. In time they had eight children. By the time Martin was 25, his father and his partners owned at least six mine shafts and two copper smelters.

Religion and Superstition

The Luthers were God-fearing people. They had devotions at home and went to church regularly. Unfortunately, like other children of his day, Martin didn't learn to know Jesus as a forgiving, loving Savior.

How did he think of Jesus? Later in life he said: "From youth I was trained to turn pale at the very mention of Christ's name. I was told to think of Him as a severe and angry Judge. We were all taught that we had to pay for our own sins. Because we could not do this, we were directed to the saints in heaven. If we prayed to dear mother Mary, maybe she could turn away Christ's anger and obtain mercy for us." As a child Martin wasn't really certain that he received mercy and forgiveness from God.

The Luthers believed many of the superstitions passed down from their ancestors. These stories told of devils, witches, and elves who played tricks and sent storms and sickness. Martin heard his mother complain that a witch caused pains in her arms and that an elf had made the milk sour. He believed these tales and was afraid of the powers of darkness and evil.

The house with the statue above the door was Luther's birthplace in Eisleben, Germany.

Corbis

Strict but Loving Parents

Like most parents in those days, Hans and Margaret Luther were very strict. Woe to Martin when he was naughty! For taking a nut without asking, his mother whipped him until he bled. Another time his father beat him so hard that Martin stayed away from him until Hans won back his love and made amends.

There was more laughter than tears, more singing than crying in the Luther home, however. Hans and Margaret loved their children and did what they thought best for them. "The best thing I received of all my father's possessions was that he educated me," Luther said years later. Martin loved his parents and respected them as God's representatives.

Martin Goes to School

Martin was not yet five years old when he started school in Mansfeld. An older boy often carried him because Martin was several years younger than other beginners.

The schools at that time were quite different from ours today. In Luther's day only boys went to school. The boys were taught to speak and read the Latin language. They knew they had to learn Latin in order to go on to the university. Churches, the law, and government all used Latin.

The priests or university students who taught them were very strict. If a boy misbehaved or didn't know his lesson, his name was written on a slate called the "wolf list." Every week the teacher erased the list after giving a blow of the rod for each time a name appeared. Martin once had a bad week—his name was on the wolf list 15 times!

Sometimes a boy would forget and speak German. If caught, he had to wear a donkey mask until he caught someone else speaking German. Of course, this meant another blow of the rod at the end of the week. The boys respected their teachers, so they took their spankings as part of school life.

Hans Luther, father of the reformer, was a copper miner and mine owner who became a member of the Mansfeld city council.

Picture-Alliance

Picture-Alliance

Martin Luther's mother, Margaret, a devout and intelligent woman, began Luther's Christian education at home.

In his early school years Martin learned the Ten Commandments, the Creed, the Lord's Prayer, the Confession of Sins, and the Hail Mary. Six times each day the beginners recited in school. At home their parents helped them learn Latin words.

By about the sixth grade Martin knew his Latin very well. He had also studied mathematics, history, speech, writing, literature, and religious music. He was trained to be a loyal church member and was ready to go on to higher schools.

11

Review Questions and Study Projects

1. Read the story and fill in the blanks.

Martin Luther was born in _____, Germany, on

_____, _____. His parents, _____ and

_____ Luther, had him _____ the very next

day.

Hans Luther made a living as a _____. He and his wife

had _____ children. Though they were very religious, the

Luthers were also _____, believing in all sorts of evil spirits.

Martin didn't learn to know Jesus as his loving _____.

Martin started school in the town of _____. Training in

school was very strict. If a boy's name appeared on the _____

_____, he was spanked. The boys learned to speak and read

_____. In beginners' school the boys were trained to be loyal

_____ members.

2. Describe how God blessed Hans Luther

a. in his family.

_____

_____

_____

b. in his work.

_____

_____

_____

c. among his neighbors.

_____

_____

_____

3. Look up Ephesians 6:1–4. Tell in your own words what it says

a. to children.

_____

_____

_____

b. to parents.

_____

_____

_____

4. Martin Luther honored his parents and teachers. To see how some people in the Bible obeyed the Fourth Commandment, look up the following passages, and fill in the blanks.

a. Genesis 47:11–12: _____ took care of his

_____.

b. 1 Kings 2:19: _____ honored his

_____.

c. 2 Kings 2:9–12: _____ honored his

_____.

d. Luke 2:51: _____ obeyed His

_____.

5. Compare young Martin Luther's ideas about Jesus with your own.

_____

_____

_____

_____

6. In what ways was Martin's school different from yours?

_____

_____

_____

_____

7. Define these words: _____

Latin _____

superstition _____

miner _____

8. Map work: On the map on page 4 place an A by the town where Martin Luther was born and a B by the city where he started school.

9. Do research to find out about St. Martin of Tours or St. Anne, the patron saint of miners. Then present a short report to your class.

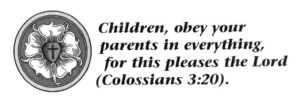
Children, obey your parents in everything, for this pleases the Lord (Colossians 3:20).

My Prayer

Dear God, thank You for giving me a home, parents, and school. Help me to love and obey my parents and teachers for Your Son's sake. Amen.

3 High School and College Days

When Martin Luther was 15, his parents sent him to Eisenach to attend the School of St. George to prepare for study at a university.

Eisenach is about 100 miles southwest of Mansfeld in a part of Germany called Thuringia. Outside its walls on a high hill stood a great stone castle, the Wartburg. Once a busy place, the Wartburg at that time was almost empty. Little did Martin know, as he first gazed up at it, that this castle would shelter him over 20 years later.

Martin was happy in the Latin school at Eisenach. The headmaster at the school, John Trebonius, and another teacher, Wiegand Geldennupf, introduced Martin to Aesop's Fables, classic literature, and history. They recognized his gifts and encouraged him to enter the university. Trebonius, especially, treated his pupils with love and respect.

One writer tells the story that whenever Master Trebonius entered his classroom, he removed his hat and bowed to the students. When asked why he did this, he answered, "Among these young pupils sit some whom God may make our future leaders and great men. Though we do not know them now, it is proper that we should honor them."

This story may not be true, but Trebonius and the other teachers at Eisenach were fine men who helped make Martin's three years there very enjoyable. In addition, they opened his eyes to the joys of learning.

A drawing of the town of Eisenach shows the Wartburg castle on top of the high hill in the center.

Corbis

14

Luther lived in the Cotta home in Eisenach when he was a student.

"Keep an Eye on That Luther"

At Eisenach Martin finished his Latin studies. He soon stood at the top of his class in speech, languages, and poetry. When Professor Trutvetter of the University of Erfurt visited the school, Martin was chosen to give a speech of welcome.

The speech pleased Trutvetter. He told Trebonius, "Keep an eye on that Luther. There is something in that boy. By all means prepare him for the university, and send him to us at Erfurt."

Turning to Martin, he said, "My son, the Lord has given you special gifts; use them faithfully in His service. When you are ready and wish to come to us at Erfurt, remember that you have a good friend there, Doctor Trutvetter. Look him up, and he will give you a kind welcome."

In the Cotta Family

In order to stay in school, the poorer students begged for food by singing in the streets. Even though his father could now pay his way, Martin liked to join the other boys in this singing. They often stopped outside the house of Kunz Cotta, a rich merchant. His wife, Ursula Cotta, had seen Martin praying in the church, and she liked his fine singing. One day she invited him into the house so he could warm himself by the fire as he ate.

Martin soon won the hearts of the Cotta family, and they took him in as a son. It so happened that Martin was giving lessons to little Henry Schalbe, a relative of Mrs. Cotta. He grew very close to these people, living with the Cottas and having his meals with the Schalbes. These families encouraged his musical talents and introduced him to a level of Christian family life and culture he had not known. Here he learned to play the flute and the lute. Johann Braun, a priest who lived in a monastery supported by these families, became a fatherly friend to Luther. With such good friends and teachers in Eisenach who shared their love of God, learning, and music with him, it is no wonder that Martin called Eisenach his "beloved town."

At the University of Erfurt

In the spring of 1501, at age 17, Martin graduated from high school. Hans Luther had always wanted his son to become a lawyer, so he sent Martin to the University of Erfurt, one of the best in Germany.

Erfurt, with over 20,000 people, was

the fifth-largest city in Germany at the time. It was sometimes called "little Rome" because of the many church-owned buildings in the city. Martin was thrilled to be in Erfurt. Here he could see and take part in many religious festivals.

The two thousand university students lived together in large buildings, about six or eight to a room. A bell rang when it was time for classes, meals, or bed. The students got up at 4 a.m. and went to bed at 8 p.m.

Like many of his university friends, Martin wore colorful clothes and carried a sword at his side. He bought a lute, a kind of guitar, and played it for songfests in his room. He also liked to hike through the lovely countryside around Erfurt.

At Erfurt Martin studied the liberal arts, which consisted of the *trivium* (grammar, dialectic or logic, and rhetoric) and the *quadrivium* (arithmetic, astronomy, geometry, and music). Dialectic was the most important because it taught Luther how to think logically. The teacher would assign a statement, or thesis, to defend. In this way students had to research their subject thoroughly, present their ideas clearly, and defend their position in debates with others. In his studies he became familiar with the writings of famous Romans and the great thinkers of Greece.

This pattern of study dates back to the days of the Greek and Roman empires. In September 1502 Luther received the Bachelor of Arts degree. He was 18.

Luther Studies Law

After two more years of hard study, Martin earned the Master of Arts degree in January 1505. One who had such a degree could teach at the university. It was a proud day for Martin and an even prouder one for his father. Hans Luther had worked hard for his son's education, and his dreams for Martin were coming true.

Martin wasn't a lawyer yet. He would begin law studies in May. Hans didn't mind the cost. His business was going

well, and he would gladly pay Martin's expenses. To encourage Martin to become a lawyer, he bought him a copy of *Corpus Juris Civilis,* an important and expensive law textbook.

Eager to please his father, Martin agreed to stay at Erfurt. He planned to teach some classes and study law at the same time. He bought a large lawbook and tried to become interested, but his heart was not in the law. At the library he spent most of his time reading other things. One book Martin discovered in the library was a Latin Bible. He loved the story of the birth of Samuel. As Luther read more, a whole new world opened to him because he had only known the Bible stories read in church.

A Change in Plans

Martin was still troubled in spirit. All his schooling hadn't changed his ideas about God and his fear of eternal punishment. He had gone to Mass and said confession faithfully. He had prayed to Mary and many other saints to help him win Jesus' mercy. Nothing had brought him spiritual comfort when he was seriously ill or when he accidentally injured himself in the leg with his sword. Deep in his heart he wasn't certain God had forgiven him.

One day in July 1505 Martin sold all his law books and invited his friends to a party. They sang and talked together as they had done many times before. As the party ended, Martin said to his friends, "Today you still see me, but never again. I am going to become a monk."

His friends were shocked. They begged and argued with him, but it was no use. He had made his decision.

The next morning some of Martin's friends went with him to the Augustinian cloister in Erfurt. The gates opened, and Martin went in. His friends returned in tears. Why should their companion, who had such a great future, throw it all away and become a monk?

God had plans for Martin Luther.

Review Questions and Study Projects

1. Read the description in Column B, and match it with a name from Column A by writing the correct letter on the blank line.

Column A
a. Ursula Cotta
b. Monastery of St. Augustine
c. Trebonius
d. Erfurt
e. Eisenach
f. Trutvetter

Column B

_____ Martin Luther went to high school here. He called it his "beloved town."

_____ The principal and teacher who treated his pupils with respect for what they might someday become.

_____ A university professor who urged Martin to use the special gifts God had given him.

_____ The wife of a rich merchant who took Martin into her home.

_____ One of Germany's largest cities, with a fine university. Here Martin earned his bachelor's and master's degrees.

_____ The place in Erfurt where a group of monks lived. Martin shocked his friends by going here.

2. Check the answer that best completes each statement.

a. Master Trebonius tipped his hat to his students because
   ☐ they were sons of rich and noble men.
   ☐ they might someday be great men.

b. When Professor Trutvetter said, "Keep an eye on that Luther," he meant
   ☐ that boy has a great future.
   ☐ that boy is dangerous.

c. Martin joined the boys in street singing because
   ☐ he was one of the poorest students.
   ☐ he loved to sing.
   ☐ he was ordered to do so by the principal.

d. Eisenach was Martin's favorite town because
   ☐ here he could watch religious festivals.
   ☐ it was close to his home in Mansfeld.
   ☐ he had close friends and good teachers there.

e. Martin studied to become a lawyer because
   ☐ his father wanted him to do this.
   ☐ lawyers were paid much money.
   ☐ he loved the study of law.

f. Martin was troubled because
   ☐ he seldom went to church.
   ☐ he wasn't sure he had done enough good to make up for his sins.

3. Matthew 9:10–13 tells how Jesus feels about sinners. Read the passage and then check the sentences you think are correct.

- [ ] Jesus seeks out and loves sinners.
- [ ] Jesus hates sinners and stays away from them.
- [ ] Jesus came only for the righteous people.
- [ ] Jesus came to call sinners to repent.

4. Luther was deeply worried about "making good" for his sins. After reading 2 Corinthians 5:19–21, write what you would say to a person with similar worries.

_____

_____

_____

_____

5. Map work: On the map on page 4 place a C by the city where Martin went to high school, his "beloved town," and a D by his university city.

6. Research and present a report to your class on one of these topics:

Aristotle   monasteries
St. Augustine   St. Benedict

7. Choose one of these theses to explain and defend. Debate it with a group of your classmates. The theses are taken from Martin Luther's Ninety-five Theses.

a. The whole life of believers must be a constant penance (Thesis 1).
b. Wrong is done to the Word of God if (the pastor) in his sermon spends as much time or more time on indulgences than on the word of the Gospel (Thesis 54).
c. Christians should be exhorted to endeavor to follow Christ their Head through Cross, Death, and Hell (Thesis 94).
d. True repentance and contrition seeks and loves punishment (Thesis 40).

8. Develop your own thesis about the Christian life to debate with your classmates. Research your thesis and present your position; then ask classmates to state and defend their positions on the thesis.

From infancy you have known the holy Scriptures, which are able to make you wise for salvation through faith in Christ Jesus (2 Timothy 3:15).

My Prayer

Dear Jesus, as I go to school, help me more and more to love God, which is the beginning of wisdom. Amen.

4 Brother Martin, Augustinian Monk

When Martin Luther entered the monastery, to his parents and friends it seemed that he had taken a giant step backward. He angered his father, shocked his teachers, saddened his friends, and apparently wasted his fine training. Why should a promising young law student make such a sudden change?

First of all, it was not as sudden a change as Martin's friends thought. Outwardly he had appeared content and happy. Inwardly, however, Martin felt his guilt as a sinner. He feared hell and purgatory and was determined to earn his salvation by living a holy life. Today we know that this is not what Scripture teaches, but in Luther's time many believed that salvation was earned by holy living.

The church had many helps to offer: sacraments, pilgrimages, and the prayers of the saints. Most people believed that the saints couldn't help if a person had done nothing to gain their favor. The best way to be sure of their aid was to become a monk. A monk could spend all of his time in religious thought, prayers, and good deeds. Martin decided that he would give himself to the Lord, as Hannah had given her son Samuel to Him.

A Growing Fear

A number of things had happened during his school years that helped Martin decide to become a monk. Once he had seen a painting of the great ship of the church. It was sailing toward heaven with only priests and monks onboard. The rest of the people were in the water and would drown unless they caught the ropes of good works thrown to them from the ship.

Luther entered the Black Cloister of the Observant Augustinians in Erfurt on July 17, 1505.

Martin remembered his reaction: "How safe and blessed to be in the ship!"

When Luther lived in the city of Magdeburg, he had seen Prince William of Anhalt dressed in monk's clothing, begging in the streets. Martin had felt ashamed of himself for not doing as much as the prince was doing to save his own soul.

Not knowing that the forgiveness for his sins was secure because of Jesus' death and resurrection, Martin was terribly afraid of death. This fear grew stronger during his college days at Erfurt. Once he accidentally cut his leg with his sword. The blood flowed fast, and the leg began to swell. Thinking he would die, he called out, "O Mary, help me!" A doctor stopped the bleeding and the leg healed, but Martin trembled whenever he thought of how close to eternal death he had been.

Another time one of Martin's close friends at Erfurt met a sudden death. Martin wondered, "What if I should die tomorrow? Would I be ready to stand before the righteous Judge of the world?"

"St. Anne, Help Me!"

With such thoughts in the back of his mind, Martin was returning to school after a visit home in July 1505. Not far from Erfurt a heavy thunderstorm came up. Lightning struck so close to him that he fell to the ground. Like many others, Martin believed lightning to be a sign of God's wrath. In terror he cried, "St. Anne, help me! I will become a monk!" He was following a well-established family prayer pattern—St. Anne was the patron saint of miners.

Later he was sorry he had made this promise, but, in spite of his friends' tears and his father's anger, he kept his word. Two weeks after the storm he entered the monastery.

The Beginning Monk

Luther chose to join a very strict group, the Augustinian Order of Hermits at Erfurt, which was noted for its vigorous academic standards and the opportunities it provided to study at the University of Erfurt. For the first two months he was closely watched. If he changed his mind, he could still leave the monastery. After a time of reflection and testing, Luther was still determined to keep his promise to St. Anne.

In a special ceremony in September 1505 Luther was made a novice, or beginner. He knelt before the prior, the man in charge of the monastery, and asked for God's grace and mercy. The prior asked him questions about his past life and reminded him that he faced a hard life. As a choir of monks sang hymns, Martin put on a white robe and a black cloak over it. The change of clothing represented a change from the old person to the new person that Luther hoped to become. A monk shaved the top of his head, an act known as tonsure. Luther was given a small black skullcap to wear at all times. He was now called Brother Martin.

During his year as a beginner Luther learned the ways of the monastery. He lived in a small, unheated cell, 7x10 feet, furnished with a table, chair, and straw bed. For exercise the monks walked in pairs around the courtyard. Seven times a day

Martin Luther was the subject of a popular black-and-white movie produced in the 1950s. Here he is pictured as a college student ladened with books and other items, passing through the Erfurt market on his way to meet friends.

In another scene from the movie *Martin Luther,* Luther is pictured begging from people in the marketplace of Erfurt. Begging was one of his duties as a priest in training.

they went to the chapel for worship.

Brother Martin, who was called Augustinus in the monastery, learned to get along on two meals a day, or only one if it was a special fast day. In his cell he spent long hours in prayer, reading, and deep thought. In this way the year as a novitiate went by, and Luther seemed to have peace of mind and soul.

After a year of training, Luther made his vows in September 1506, and he became a monk. He promised that he would remain poor, never marry, and would obey God and the leaders in the monastery. He lay flat on the floor, spreading out his arms in the form of a cross. The prior sprinkled him with holy water, and the choir sang sad songs for the death of the old man and joyful songs for the birth of the new. Martin arose, a full-fledged monk.

The Young Priest

Shortly after this, Luther was chosen to become a priest. For eight or nine months he studied books that explained the sacraments, and on May 2, 1507, he officiated at his first Communion, or Mass.

For this special event Luther invited his father, who had not written to him for a year. Hans Luther wrote that he would come, though he was still unhappy about his son's decision. By this time Hans was doing very well. He arrived with 20 horsemen, and he gave the monastery $300 to help pay the expenses of the celebration.

At dinner Martin told his father how God had called him in the storm and led him to become a monk. Hans snapped back, "God grant that it was not the devil's trick! Have you never read that you should honor your father and your mother?" Luther's father was still concerned that his family would not be taken care of after his death because Martin had chosen to become a monk. Martin remembered his father's comment throughout his life.

The young priest trembled when he held his first Mass. As he said the words "We offer to You, the living, the true, the eternal God," he wondered how he, a sinner, dared speak to the great and holy God. He was so afraid that he was hardly able to finish the service.

Here lay Luther's big problem. God is perfectly holy and demands holiness of all who come into His presence. Luther knew he was sinful. How then could he be saved?

Martin knew the church's answers: One was confession—telling a priest one's sins and hearing him say they are forgiven. Another answer was to become a monk, doing good works to please God. These answers didn't quiet Luther's soul. Had he remembered *all* his sins in the confession? Had he done *enough* good works to win God's favor? He anguished over these thoughts, and at times he felt not love, but hatred, toward a God who would cause him such misery.

21

Review Questions and Study Projects

1. Read each sentence carefully. If the sentence is true, circle the T. If it is false, circle the F.

   T   F   a. Martin's friends and family were glad that he became a monk.

   T   F   b. By entering the monastery, Luther hoped to please God and the saints.

   T   F   c. Monks promised to remain poor and never marry.

   T   F   d. The life of the Augustinian monks was happy and carefree.

   T   F   e. After a year as a beginner, Martin took his final vows as a monk.

   T   F   f. Luther's father refused to come to the monastery for Martin's first Mass.

   T   F   g. No one can earn salvation by doing good works.

   T   F   h. Jesus is a kind, loving, and forgiving Savior.

2. This paragraph reviews a number of things that led Martin Luther to enter a monastery. Fill in the blanks.

Once Martin had seen a painting of the great _____ of the church. Only if people caught the ropes of _____ _____ thrown by the churchmen onboard could they be saved. Luther had also seen a _____ begging in the streets, and he wanted to do as much for his own _____. Martin's fear of _____ became stronger after he cut himself with his _____ and after a good _____ died. In _____, near Erfurt, a flash of _____ in a storm frightened him into promising to become a monk.

3. As a young man, Luther believed the only way to God was through saints and good works. Read John 14:6 and write in your own words what it tells you.

_____

_____

_____

_____

_____

4. Define these words:

fast day _____

confession _____

5. Complete the crossword puzzle on the next page.

Across

1. During a storm Martin called on this saint to help him.
2. The city where Martin entered a monastery.
4. Martin tried to please Him by good works.
5. The _____ was celebrated instead of Holy Communion.
7. "We offer to You, the living, the _____, the eternal God."
9. Shaving the top of a monk's head.
12. When Luther became this, he could preach and say the Mass.
13. A beginner; Martin was this for his first year in the monastery.
14. One who lives in a monastery.

Down

1. Luther joined the _____ Order of Hermits.
3. To go without food for a time.
6. Martin hurt this with his sword.
8. Head of a monastery.
10. Luther tried to remember and confess every ___.
11. As a monk, Luther was called "Brother ___."

6. Pretend you are Luther shortly after entering the monastery. Write a letter to your father explaining your reasons for becoming a monk. Remember that this decision was a surprise and a disappointment to Hans Luther.

This righteousness from God comes through faith in Jesus Christ to all who believe. There is no difference, for all have sinned and fall short of the glory of God, and are justified freely by His grace through the redemption that came by Christ Jesus (Romans 3:22–24).

My Prayer

Dear Father, I am glad that all my sins are forgiven because Jesus died for me. Through Your Holy Spirit, help me live a life of service to You and people everywhere. Amen.

5 "Greetings to You, Holy Rome!"

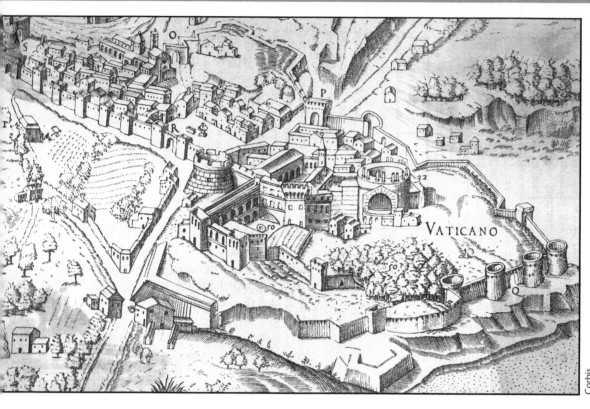

A sixteenth-century woodcut of Rome, the "Holy City," provides a picture of what Luther saw when he visited there in 1511.

Corbis

Martin Luther couldn't stay away from school for long. Shortly after he became a priest, he began attending classes at the University of Erfurt. This time he studied religion instead of law. He wanted to be able to teach the Bible to others, but he was also seeking peace for himself. Unfortunately, his study of the religious thought of the mystics such as Thomas à Kempis and Johannes Tauler, who taught that salvation could be gained through meditation, or the humanists such as Erasmus, who taught that a person could improve by reading good literature about people, brought him no peace. They all taught that people had to work hard and persevere to be saved.

In 1508, after Luther had studied a

year, John Staupitz visited him. Dr. Staupitz, head of all the Augustinian monks in Germany, wanted Luther to teach philosophy at the new University of Wittenberg and to pursue his doctoral degree.

After hours of discussion, Staupitz, in effect, ordered Martin to move to Wittenberg, where he was to teach and begin doctoral studies. In spring 1509 he received permission to teach classes on the Bible. As Luther taught from the Bible, he was more and more drawn into the book. In this way God was preparing His servant for the great work that lay ahead.

"I Did Not Know Christ"

But the servant as yet didn't really know his Master. Luther himself later said,

Luther in his room.

"I did not believe in Christ except as a stern and terrible Judge. That is why I turned to Mary and the saints and my own good works. It was all a false religion and idolatry because I did not know Christ, and my works were not done out of faith in Him."

Instead of praying to Christ, Luther prayed to Mary and the saints. He prayed to 21 saints, three of them each day of the week. He tried all sorts of things to please God by controlling his body, including whipping and starving himself, praying all night without sleeping, and locking himself in his room for several days. In spite of these efforts, he still didn't feel he was doing enough to earn God's love.

One day, when Martin was quite discouraged, a fellow priest cheered him up by reminding him of these words of the Apostles' Creed: "I believe in the forgiveness of sins." The priest asked him, "Isn't the God who gave His only Son a loving, merciful God? Didn't Jesus' death pay for all sins?" These words brought Luther some relief, and he never forgot them.

Staupitz, too, tried to encourage Luther. When Martin said his sins were too great, Staupitz told him, "Christ is the for-

giveness for all sins. He is a real Savior. God has sent His own Son and delivered Him up for us." Luther said later that without Staupitz at his side he would have given up in despair.

Luther Goes to Rome

In the fall of 1510 some welcome news came to Luther. He was to go to Rome! A quarrel had started among the Augustinians about a new set of rules for monks to live by. Luther and another monk were to ask the leaders in Rome to settle the quarrel.

Imagine Luther's excitement as he thought about the trip. Rome was then, as it still is, the center of interest and authority for the Roman Catholic Church. The pope himself lived there. Except for Palestine, Rome contained more holy places and relics than any other place on earth. Wouldn't it offer just the medicine for Luther's spiritual sickness?

The two monks walked the 850 miles south to Rome in about seven weeks. They ate and slept in monasteries along the way. After crossing the Alps, they traveled through northern Italy. Finally, one day in January 1511, they saw Rome in the distance. Luther fell to the ground and cried, "Greetings to you, holy Rome!"

Once the leading city of the world, Rome had only about 40,000 people at this time. Ruins of ancient Roman buildings were everywhere, but Luther didn't care about seeing these signs of Rome's former glory. He wanted to visit as many churches and sacred places and see as many relics as possible. The discussions of the monastery's concerns took only a little of his time. The rest of the time he spent as a pilgrim in the holy city.

Sad Conditions in Rome

There was much for a Christian to see in Rome: the stairway Jesus climbed at His trial before Pilate, 11 thorns from Jesus' crown, a piece of the cross and one of the nails that held Jesus to it, branches from the burning bush of Moses, one of Judas's 30 pieces of silver, the table of the Last Supper, crumbs of the loaves that fed 5,000, and many other relics. Luther believed they all were genuine. He thought that touching and kissing the relics or praying before them were good works. Such works, he had been taught, could reduce a person's stay in purgatory by many years.

In fact, Luther believed the common notion that if a person did more good works than necessary for himself, he could "lend" some to others who were already in purgatory. Talking about his trip to Rome, he later said, "I felt sorry that my parents were still living, for I would have liked to free them from purgatory by masses and good works."

Much of what he saw and heard in Rome shocked Luther. Many of the Italian priests were poorly educated, and they made fun of sacred things. Some of the highest church leaders lived wicked lives.

Corbis

While in Rome, Luther may have stayed in the monastery of this church, Santa Maria del Popolo.

Later Martin told of the doubts that began entering his mind. "While in Rome I wished to free my grandfather from purgatory," he wrote. "I went up the stairway of Pilate, where Jesus had been led. On my hands and knees I prayed on each step and kissed it for good measure. But when I came to the top, I thought, 'Who knows whether this is true?' "

Luther still believed the only way to heaven was through the church, but he wondered whether the church was being true to God and His Word. He knew that personal peace could not be obtained by doing acts of obedience. With these mixed feelings Luther returned to Germany.

Review Questions and Study Projects

1. Complete the sentences by underlining the correct word or group of words.

a. Luther went back to the university to study (law, religion).

b. Luther studied and taught at the universities of (Erfurt and Wittenberg, Leipzig and Cologne).

c. The head of the Augustinians, who did much to encourage Luther, was (Spalatin, Staupitz).

d. Luther was sent to Rome (to find peace for his soul, to ask officials to settle a dispute among the Augustinians).

e. When Luther saw the relics in Rome (he believed they were genuine, he knew they were only copies of the real things).

f. Luther climbed (Jacob's ladder, Pilate's stairway) in order to free his (mother, grandfather) from purgatory.

2. Check the statements that tell what Luther did to try to please God.

_____ a. Prayed all night without sleeping

_____ b. Threw himself completely on God's mercy

_____ c. Whipped and starved himself

_____ d. Prayed to Mary and the saints

_____ e. Asked forgiveness for Jesus' sake

_____ f. Locked himself in his room for days

3. Luther said that his works were not done out of faith in Christ. Read Hebrews 11:6. Summarize its message in your own words.

_____

_____

_____

_____

_____

4. Why can't a person be saved by the extra good works of others? See Ephesians 2:8–9.

_____

_____

_____

_____

_____

5. What doubts did Luther have about the church after he had been in Rome?

_____

_____

_____

_____

_____

Why did he have these doubts?

_____

_____

_____

_____

6. Map work: On the map on page 4 use a colored pencil to draw a line from Erfurt to Rome that passes through the following cities: Nuremberg, Augsburg, Milan, Florence, Rome. Luther probably followed this route on his trip to Rome.

7. Some of the world's finest religious art was produced in Italy at the time of Luther's visit to Rome. Gather information and then present a short report on the work of one of the following artists:
Brunelleschi
Michelangelo
Leonardo da Vinci
Raphael

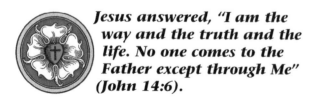

Jesus answered, "I am the way and the truth and the life. No one comes to the Father except through Me" **(John 14:6).**

My Prayer

Merciful Father in heaven, thank You for sending Jesus to save me from my sins. Teach me never to look to anyone but Jesus for forgiveness and salvation. Amen.

6 Gates of Paradise

October 19, 1512, was a big day in Wittenberg. The bells rang out joyfully as professors and students from the university marched through the streets toward the collegiate Castle Church of All Saints.

During the ceremony in church all eyes were on a pale, thin monk. Dr. Andreas Karlstadt read some Bible verses. Then Martin Luther vowed to teach only true doctrine and report on anyone who taught falsely. Karlstadt placed a woolen cap on the monk's head and slipped a silver ring on his finger. Martin Luther was now a Doctor of Theology.

A few days later he succeeded Dr. Staupitz as professor of the Bible at the University of Wittenberg. Luther would hold this position for the remaining 34 years of his life.

Persuaded by Staupitz

Luther hadn't planned to become a professor. After his return to Erfurt from Rome, Luther and his friend John Lang announced that they agreed with the decision made in Rome that all Augustinian monasteries should be under the authority of John Staupitz, the vicar general for Germany. This was not the decision hoped for by the majority of monks of the Black Cloister in Erfurt. Because of this disagreement, Luther and Lang moved to Wittenberg to join Dr. Staupitz at the university. Here Luther lived in the Augustinian monastery, as he had in Erfurt.

The Castle Church at Wittenberg was the scene of many activities connected with the reformation.

Picture-Alliance

29

Shortly afterward Staupitz asked Luther to become a preacher and to study for the Doctor of Theology degree. Luther at once objected, "But so much work would kill me!"

Staupitz replied, "God has much work to be done. Even if you die, you can help Him in heaven."

Staupitz was looking for teachers for the University of Wittenberg. He knew Luther would make a good one. He also knew Luther was struggling with spiritual questions. Staupitz thought that perhaps Luther would forget his own troubles if he spent more time helping other people find relief from theirs. Perhaps Luther would find peace in the Bible, for he would need to study it in his new position.

At Wittenberg the teachers thought highly of Luther. One older professor said, "This monk will start a new religion and reform the whole Roman Church. Why? Because he stands on the words of Christ, which no learning can overthrow."

Time passed quickly for Luther. Preaching to the monks, instructing the beginners in the monastery, and studying the Bible kept him very busy. When Luther was made a doctor and professor, Staupitz gave up his own position as lecturer in the Bible so that Luther could have it.

A Great Discovery

In his first few years as a professor Dr. Luther taught lessons from Genesis, Psalms, Romans, Galatians, and Hebrews. He spent much time studying the Scriptures in order to prepare his lectures. Many evenings when all else was dark at the monastery a light still shone from Luther's study in the tower.

One such evening in 1514 he made a great discovery. He was working on his notes from the Book of Psalms. The psalmist had prophesied Jesus' words on the cross: "My God, My God, why have You forsaken Me?"

Luther was puzzled. Why should the holy Son of God feel forsaken by His Father? Luther knew that he himself felt just this way many times, but he also knew he was a sinner, while Jesus was pure and sinless. The only answer had to be that Christ took our sins on Himself.

Surely the God who did this for us is a merciful God!

Yet God is not only merciful, but also just and righteous. How many times Luther had stumbled over the phrase "the righteousness of God"! To him that meant that God shows His righteousness by punishing sinners. He feared those words.

Luther was now a doctor of theology.

Luther struggled as he studied God's Word. Here he is pictured in the opera *Luther* by Kari Tikka, produced in 2001 in Minneapolis. The Holy Spirit led Luther to an understanding of "the righteousness of God."

Since the apostle Paul often mentioned the righteousness of God, Luther turned to Paul's letters, trying to understand the phrase. In Romans 1:17 he read, "In the gospel a righteousness from God is revealed, a righteousness that is by faith from first to last, just as it is written: 'The righteous will live by faith.' "

It wasn't easy for Luther to forget what he had been taught all his life, but finally he saw the real meaning of the phrase "the righteousness of God." God's righteousness was not the goodness that God Himself has, but the goodness God gives to us. This righteousness is not a reward for any good a person has done. Rather it is a free gift to all who believe that Jesus suffered and died in their place for their sins.

The Gates Open

How excited Luther was! "I felt exactly as though I had been born again," he reported. "Before this I had hated the words 'righteousness of God.' Now I loved them. These words of the apostle Paul opened the gates of Paradise for me!"

For the first time in his life Luther could feel certain his sins were forgiven. Christ was no longer the angry Judge. To Luther He was now the kind, gracious Savior who said, "Come to Me, all you who are weary and burdened, and I will give you rest" (Matthew 11:28).

Martin Luther would never let go of this doctrine of justification by faith. *Sola fide*—"faith alone"—became Luther's motto. To this day it is one of the central teachings of the Lutheran church.

Review Questions and Study Projects

1. Complete these sentences by writing in the correct word or words on each line. Choose words from the list.

loving and merciful	took on Himself
punishing sinners	God's Word professor
trust forsaken	His righteousness
St. Paul	were forgiven peace

a. Staupitz wanted Luther to become
a _____ at the University of Wittenberg.

b. Staupitz hoped that Luther might find _____
by studying and teaching the Bible.

c. Luther based his religious teachings on
_____.

d. On the cross Jesus was _____ by God.

e. Though Jesus was holy, He _____ the
sins of all people.

f. God sent Jesus to save us because God is
_____.

g. Luther thought "the righteousness of God" meant His justice in
_____.

h. When Jesus took our sins on Himself, He covered us with
_____.

i. To receive God's free gift of forgiveness, we
_____ in Jesus as our Savior.

j. In the writings of _____ Luther found the Good
News of the Gospel.

k. After his "tower discovery" Luther was sure his sins
_____.

2. Look up Romans 10:10. Tell in your own words how a person is justified, or made righteous, in God's sight.

_____

_____

3. Read John 3:16 and answer the following questions.
a. What did God do for the world?

_____

_____

b. Why did He do this?

_____

_____

c. How do you receive eternal life?

_____

_____

4. Read 2 Corinthians 5:21. Fill in the blanks to explain the meaning of this Bible verse. Use the words below. (Some may be used more than once.)

God	righteous	sin	Jesus	people

_____ made _____ to be _____ for all

_____, even though _____ was without

_____. Because of this, all _____ who

believe in _____ become _____ before

_____.

5. You can be sure that your sins are forgiven. Tell what this means to you and how it makes you feel.

_____

_____

6. Define these words:

theology _____

righteousness _____

forsaken _____

professor _____

7. Map work: On the map on page 4 place an E before the city where Luther lived and taught for much of his life.

8. Research and present a report to your class on one of the following topics:
   John Staupitz (1469–1524)
   St. Augustine
   University of Wittenberg

The righteous will live by faith (Romans 1:17).

My Prayer

Dear Jesus, how can I thank You enough for dying for my sins? Keep my faith strong through Your Holy Spirit as long as I live. Amen.

7 Indulgences for Sale

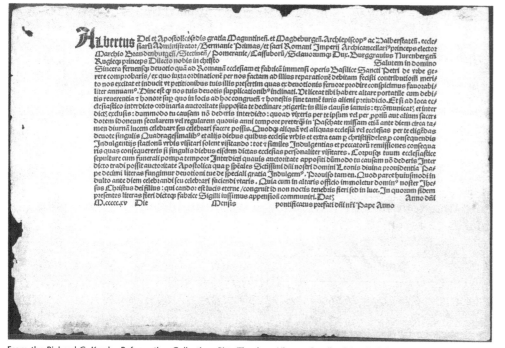

From the Richard C. Kessler Reformation Collection, Pitts Theology Library, Candler School of Theology, Emory University

This indulgence letter from Brandenburg was used by John Tetzel. Only the name of the person and the date needed to be written in the blanks.

in purgatory. Cleansing in purgatory was thought to be very painful and had to last a long time.

The Treasury of Merits

As a way to escape suffering in purgatory, the church taught that people could draw on the "treasury of merits." According to this teaching, Jesus and some saints had done many more good works than they themselves needed. These extra good works were stored in a heavenly treasury. The church could transfer some of these merits to the sinner by granting an indulgence. When enough indulgences were purchased on behalf of a person, the soul of the person, living or dead, could be freed from purgatory.

The church did not say that indulgences gave forgiveness of sins. A person who bought or earned an indulgence still had to confess his or her sins to a priest and receive forgiveness. To a good many people, however, release from sin's punishment was the same as forgiveness of the sin.

The church at Luther's time taught that there were two kinds of punishment for sins: eternal and temporal. The eternal penalty was hell. To escape hell, the sinner had to repent of his sins with all his heart.

The temporal penalty had two parts: "satisfaction" on earth and "cleansing" in purgatory.

The earthly satisfaction for sin was set by the church. When someone confessed a sin, the priest told the person what to do to make up for it. The "satisfaction," or penalty, might be giving up a certain food, giving money for some church project, or saying certain prayers many times.

Since these good works covered only a part of the penalty for the sins a person had committed, more cleansing was needed

Special agents sold indulgence letters all over Europe. The letters contained the pope's signature and seal. One of the indulgence sellers was John Tetzel, a monk. To understand what he was doing, we must look back a few years.

Albert the Archbishop

In 1513 the archbishop of the city of Mainz died. Albert of Brandenburg wanted to be the next archbishop. This would make him the leading church official in Germany.

Albert, however, was only 23, too young to be an archbishop. He needed special permission from the pope, and this would cost much money. Other men also wanted the office of archbishop, so Albert would have to pay more than any of them. When he offered $250,000 more than the regular payment of $300,000, Pope Leo X said, "Albert is the only man for the job."

Albert had to borrow the money from bankers. To enable him to repay his debt, the pope issued a papal bull allowing indulgences to be sold in Germany. Half of the money would go to build St. Peter's Church in Rome. The other half would go to Albert to repay the bankers.

Tetzel the Salesman

Albert himself did not sell the indulgences, but he hired a number of salesmen. John Tetzel was the one chosen to work near Wittenberg.

Tetzel was a good salesman. As with a modern circus, his coming was announced in a town weeks ahead of time. He sent men ahead to find out how much money each person

in the town earned. The rich would be expected to pay more for their indulgences than the poor.

Big crowds met Tetzel when he arrived. He began with a sermon on "Hell," vividly showing the agony of the unbelievers. Next came his sermon on "Purgatory." It pictured relatives and dear ones crying out for relief from their suffering. His last sermon, on "Heaven," told of the peace and happiness in Paradise. After hearing these sermons the people were ready to buy indulgences.

Luther Speaks Out

When Luther heard of all this, he was shocked. He had preached against indulgences before, warning that they could not take the place of repentance and sorrow for sin. Now he realized that indulgences were being sold under the guise that they had the power to give complete forgiveness of sins. Some of Luther's members, after hearing Tetzel, came for confession and said they were not sorry for their sins.

Picture-Alliance

John Tetzel, the monk who sold indulgences near Wittenberg, is pictured in this 1727 engraving.

A large portion of the indulgence money was used to pay for work on the magnificent St. Peter's Basilica in Rome. The church, one of the largest Christian churches in the world, is said to contain the tomb of St. Peter. It took more than 200 years to plan and complete the building. The artist Michelangelo designed the beautiful dome, which soars to a height of 400 feet.

Corbis

Instead, they waved their indulgence letters in Luther's face and claimed that their sins were completely forgiven and there was no need for confession and contrition. Martin refused to give them absolution or Holy Communion until they were penitent. In a sermon that he preached one year before he nailed the Ninety-five Theses to the door at Wittenberg, he emphasized the importance of sincere repentance. "Contrition lasts throughout the Christian's life," he said. No indulgence could replace true repentance.

During the next year Luther preached still stronger sermons against indulgences. In doing this he risked the anger of Frederick the Wise, an important ruler in the part of Germany called Saxony.

Frederick's Castle Church of All Saints in Wittenberg held a huge collection of relics that Frederick had carefully gathered over many years. Each year on November 1, All Saints' Day, he displayed them so that anyone who saw these relics and left a gift in the church was granted an indulgence that removed two million years from his or her stay in purgatory. The money went for the support of the Wittenberg church and university. Despite Luther's sermons, members of his congregation continued to buy indulgences.

Luther liked his position at the university, and he loved and respected his ruler, but he cared more about the spiritual health of God's people. Luther could not stand by and do nothing. Besides, All Saints' Day was drawing near, and huge crowds would be seeking indulgences at the Castle Church. The time had come to take a stronger step.

Review Questions and Study Projects

1. Check the sentences that tell what the church in Luther's day taught about sin and its punishment:

____ a. There is one penalty for sin, the eternal penalty of hell.

____ b. "Satisfaction" and purgatory are parts of the temporal punishment for sins.

____ c. Each sinner decides what his own satisfaction for sins will be.

____ d. Most people can do enough good works to cover all their sins.

____ e. The extra good works of Christ and the saints can be transferred to people on earth.

____ f. By granting indulgences the church can free souls from purgatory.

____ g. Indulgences can be given only by God.

____ h. Indulgences can be used for dead people as well as living people.

2. The following words could have been spoken by one of the persons or the group listed in the box. Decide which person or group the words best fit, and write the name on the line. Some names may be used more than once.

Luther	Frederick the Wise	Tetzel
Albert	Pope Leo X	Luther's members

_____ a. "Remember, the university is supported by gifts from people who see my relics. If they don't come, you may be out of a job."

_____ b. "God looks at the heart. If you are not sorry for your sins, an indulgence paper, even though signed by the pope, is worthless."

_____ c. "As soon as the coin clinks in the chest, the soul flies up to heavenly rest."

_____ d. "What does it matter if we sin? We have indulgences signed by the pope himself."

_____ e. "If he can gather that much money, he is just the man we need in Germany. Let him be the new archbishop."

_____ f. "By His suffering and death Christ obtained full forgiveness for all your sins. Only believe and repent with all your heart, and forgiveness is yours."

_____ g. "The pope needs money badly. If I offer him enough, he will close his eyes to the rules."

_____ h. "Do you not hear your dear parents crying out, 'Have mercy on us. For a small amount you can set us free'?"

3. What would you say to a person who told you that forgiveness of sins can be earned or bought?

_____

_____

_____

4. Read Isaiah 53:4–6. What does this passage tell you about the punishment for sins?

_____

_____

_____

5. Read the following Bible passages. Then check the statement below each one that is true.

    a. Romans 3:10–12

      _____ No one can live a sinless life.

      _____ The saints are righteous before God because of their holy life.

    b. Luke 16:19–31

      _____ After death, souls go to purgatory for cleansing.

      _____ After death, a person goes to heaven or to hell.

    c. Luke 18:10–14

      _____ God forgives those who are sorry for their sins and trust in Him for mercy.

      _____ A person must lead a good life before God will forgive his sins.

6. Define these words:

    temporal   indulgence   satisfaction   archbishop
      merits   absolution   contrition

7. Map work: On the map on page 4 place an F by the city of Mainz.

8. Research and prepare a presentation on one of the following topics:

John Tetzel   St. Peter's Basilica

Albert of Mainz   Castle Church of All Saints in Wittenberg

Michelangelo

He was pierced for our transgressions, He was crushed for our iniquities; the punishment that brought us peace was upon Him, and by His wounds we are healed (Isaiah 53:5).

My Prayer

Merciful Father in heaven, I sin daily and deserve Your punishment. I am truly sorry for them, and I repent of all my sins. Forgive them for the sake of Your Son, Jesus, who took on Himself the punishment I deserved. Amen.

8 The Ninety-five Theses

On October 31 many people celebrate Halloween. In the church, October 31 is All Hallows' Eve or the Eve of All Saints' Day. Many Lutheran Christians observe the same day as Reformation Day. It is no accident that these two observances are celebrated on the same day, as we will see in this lesson.

The door of the Castle Church in Wittenberg on which Luther posted his Ninety-five Theses burned. It was replaced by this door, which has an engraving of the theses on it.

Corbis

Several times in 1516 and 1517 Martin Luther had preached against the selling of indulgences. This took courage, for John Tetzel had been given power by Pope Leo X to excommunicate those who spoke against this activity.

Luther was not afraid. He knew that St. Augustine had never mentioned indulgences. Others before him had spoken against indulgences. Then, too, Tetzel was making claims for his indulgences that had never been made before. Luther thought the church leaders didn't really know what Tetzel was doing. He was sure that when they found out, they would stop the evil business. Luther loved his church and was simply trying to defend it against a false teacher.

The recently invented printing press helped to spread Luther's ideas rapidly.

Most important, Luther knew what God wanted him to do. Buying indulgences kept many people from relying completely on the forgiveness they had in Christ. Luther remembered that he himself knew the comfort of the Gospel only after many years of living in spiritual darkness. Now he must spread the light of the Gospel wherever and whenever he could.

By October 1517 Tetzel had left the Wittenberg area, but All Saints' Day, November 1, was fast approaching. Crowds of people would seek indulgence by viewing Frederick the Wise's relics, among them a thorn from the crown of Christ, according to the catalog of the collection of relics. So Luther went to work in his tower room. He planned to take advantage of the opportunity to publicize his views.

The Writing on the Door

Let's imagine how it happened: It is All Saints' Eve, October 31, 1517, the day before All Saints' Day. People are beginning to gather in Wittenberg's streets, waiting for church services to begin.

Around noon a monk, wearing the cap and ring of a professor, and his teaching assistant Johann Schneider leave the Augustinian monastery and walk through the marketplace. The monk, Martin Luther, steps to the door of the Castle Church, unrolls a large sheet of paper, and nails it to the north door. Then the two slip away as bystanders press closer to see what the paper says.

The paper is written in Latin. As more people gather around, some who can read it translate it into German for others to hear. It begins with these words:

"Out of love for the truth the following theses will be debated at Wittenberg, the Reverend Father Martin Luther, Master of Arts and Sacred Theology, presiding. He begs that those who cannot attend the oral discussion will send their ideas in writing. In the name of our Lord Jesus Christ. Amen."

Then followed Luther's Ninety-five Theses, or sentences, that he wanted to debate.

1. When our Lord and Master Jesus Christ said, "Repent," He intended the entire life of believers to be one of repentance.

32. All who believe that letters of pardon make them sure of salvation will be lost eternally, together with their teachers.

36. Every Christian who truly repents of his sins is fully free from punishment and guilt without indulgence letters.

62. The true treasure of the church is the holy Gospel of the glory and grace of God.

82. If the pope lets souls out of purgatory for the sake of money, why doesn't he do it for the sake of holy love?

There were three main points in Luther's attack on the selling of indulgences. First, he said that the entire life of a Christian should be one of repentance. Second, he was certain that indulgences did not give forgiveness of sins; this comes only through sorrow for sins and faith in Christ. Christians should be urged to follow Christ their Head through cross, death, and hell (Thesis 94). Third, he claimed that buying indulgences was harmful to the Christian life. Every person who feels sincere repentance and woe for his sins has perfect remission of punishment and guilt (Thesis 36). Indulgences made people feel that Christian living wasn't important. "He who gives to the poor or lends to a needy man does better than he who buys an indulgence" (Thesis 43), Luther wrote.

The Church Begins to Act

Luther's theses were translated from Latin and printed in German. Using the recently invented (circa 1450) printing

Where in the picture do you see Frederick the Wise sleeping and dreaming? What burning is taking place? Luther appears twice in the dream. What is he doing each time? What is Luther's long pen doing on each end? What guidance is given to Luther and Frederick? What is the message of this cartoon?

CPH

press of Johann Gutenberg that used movable type, Luther's supporters reprinted the Niney-five Theses. Soon they had spread all over Europe. His theses were the focus of the first great media event in the new communication age. Many people cheered Luther for daring to speak the truth. Others, for various reasons, wanted to silence him.

Archbishop Albert of Mainz, who wanted the income from the sale of indulgences, was one who wanted to silence Luther. He sent a copy of the theses to Rome and asked the pope to stop Luther from preaching or writing any more about indulgences. The pope didn't seem too worried at first. It was just the monks having another one of their quarrels, he said. If he did nothing, the whole thing would be forgotten.

Tetzel also wanted Luther stopped. After Luther's attack, indulgence sales dropped off sharply. Tetzel's first move was to threaten Luther with burning at the stake. When that didn't work, he asked his order of monks, the Dominicans, to help him. They appealed to the leaders in Rome to halt the spread of Luther's dangerous teachings.

Now the church leaders at Rome began to act. The head of the Augustinian Order demanded that John Staupitz solve the "Luther problem." The German Augustinians held a meeting at Heidelberg in April 1518. Despite warnings that his life was in danger, Luther went to this meeting, walking the 270 miles from Wittenberg to Heidelberg.

In a debate with the professors from the University of Heidelberg, Luther skillfully defended his ideas about grace, faith, sin, and free will. In the words of one listener, "His answers, so brief, so wise, and drawn from the Holy Scriptures, easily made all his hearers his admirers."

The Augustinians did not order Luther to stop preaching and writing. Instead, they asked him to explain his theses more fully in writing. When Luther did this, they sent copies to the pope.

Luther returned to Wittenberg in triumph. God had protected him from all dangers and had given him good friends. He was not alone in his fight.

41

Review Questions and Study Projects

1. Read each sentence carefully. If the sentence is true, circle the T. If it is false, circle the F.

T F a. Both Reformation Day and Halloween are on October 31.

T F b. Luther was the first person to speak against indulgences.

T F c. None of the church leaders knew what Tetzel was doing.

T F d. In preaching against indulgences, Luther knew he was doing what God wanted him to do.

T F e. Once Tetzel left the Wittenberg area, there was no more danger of people wanting an indulgence.

T F f. Luther's Ninety-five Theses were some ideas on indulgences that he wished to debate with others.

T F g. In the theses Luther attacked the selling of indulgences.

T F h. The pope did not try to silence Luther right away.

T F i. Albert of Mainz and Tetzel thought Luther was right in attacking indulgences.

T F j. Staupitz and the Augustinians did not order Luther to stop preaching and teaching.

T F k. Luther was not allowed to debate or discuss his ideas at Heidelberg.

2. Why is October 31 called "All Hallows' Eve"?

_____

_____

Why is it also called "Reformation Day"?

_____

_____

3. What were Luther's three main arguments against indulgences?

_____

_____

4. Explain what the first of Luther's theses means to you by naming specific ways in which you can live a life of repentance.

_____

_____

_____

5. Look up the following Bible passages and answer the questions.
   a. Matthew 23:13–15. How were indulgence sellers like the scribes and Pharisees?

   _____

   _____

   b. Acts 8:18–22. Look up the word *simony* in a dictionary. How does simony relate to this story?

   _____

   _____

   Which words of Peter's reply to Simon would best fit the indulgence sellers?

   _____

   _____

   Which words are almost the same as Luther's advice to his people?

   _____

   _____

   c. Luke 19:45–48. Compare this incident in Jesus' life with Luther's posting of the Ninety-five Theses.

   _____

   _____

6. Map work: On the map on page 4 place a G near Heidelberg.

7. Very important to the spread of Luther's ideas was the printing press. Use an encyclopedia to make a report on this invention. Make a drawing of the kind of press used in Luther's time.

8. Research and present a report on one of the following people:

   Johann Gutenberg

   John Eck

   Philip Melanchthon

   Pope Leo X

In [Jesus] we have redemption through His blood, the forgiveness of sins, in accordance with the riches of God's grace that He lavished on us with all wisdom and understanding (Ephesians 1:7–8).

My Prayer

Thank You, dear God, for the faithful pastors and teachers who have taught me Your Word. Give me the strength and courage to defend the Gospel treasure that is mine and to share it with others. In Jesus' name I pray. Amen.

9 The Church Tries to Silence Luther

Many people were glad that Luther had attacked the indulgence business, but others hated him for it. Some of Tetzel's Dominican friends spread lies about Luther. Emperor Maximilian I heard and believed these lies. He wrote the pope, urging him to do something about Luther.

Lies, however, were not needed to get the church to take action against Luther. This "shabby little monk" had attacked indulgences, one of the church's biggest money-making activities. Besides, the pope had approved indulgences, so Luther was really attacking the pope!

To make matters worse, Luther had preached a strong sermon about excommunication to prepare the people of Wittenberg if they were threatened with excommunication if they did not buy indulgences. In it he had said that an excommunicated person, if he still had faith in his heart, could go to heaven. If people began believing this, the church would lose its greatest power over them. Pope Leo X knew that. Now he began to move against the reformer.

First, Luther was told to appear in Rome for "examination." Then the pope changed the orders and told Cardinal Cajetan to arrest

Corbis

Leo X, pope from 1513 to 1521, was the son of Lorenzo the Magnificent of Florence. He increased papal income and wanted to enjoy the papal office. This picture of Leo X and the cardinals was painted by Raphael.

Corbis

A bronze statue of Frederick the Wise, ruler of Saxony in Luther's time, shows him as a defender of his lands and people.

Luther" before he spread his ideas too far.

Luther was in great danger. The Dominicans, his own Augustinian general, a cardinal, the pope, and the emperor were all lined up against him.

Frederick Protects Luther

God, however, provided Luther with a powerful protector—Elector Frederick the Wise of Saxony. Frederick thought highly of his professor of religion. Many of his officials, including court preacher George Spalatin, were on Luther's side, and they spoke well of him to Frederick. The elector was determined that Luther would have a fair trial. Frederick knew that if Luther were ever lured into one of the territories of the opposition and captured, he would never receive a fair trial, so Frederick cleverly stalled all attempts to have Luther travel in areas not under his protection.

Frederick could disobey both pope and emperor at this time because the Turks were again moving deep into Europe. The pope would need the help of every Christian prince to fight the Turks, so he could not afford to have a serious quarrel with a man such as Frederick. In addition, Emperor Maximilian was old and feeble. When he died, Frederick was one of the seven princes who would elect a new emperor. The pope needed Frederick's vote to elect the man he wanted to be the next emperor. As a result, when Frederick asked that Luther be allowed to defend himself before a fair judge in Germany, the pope agreed. The emperor had called for a diet to meet in Augsburg. A diet was a gathering of political representatives from all over the empire. They met frequently to make governmental decisions. They gathered in Augsburg to discuss financing the war against the Turks and, Maximilian hoped, to assure the election of his grandson, Charles I of Spain and Naples, to succeed him as emperor. Cardinal Cajetan promised to meet Luther during the diet in Augsburg and to deal with him in a "fatherly manner."

Luther. "When you have Martin in your power," the pope wrote, "keep him under a safe guard until you hear further from us." The pope also said that if Luther repented of his attacks, he should be released; if not, the church would punish him with excommunication.

Another order from the pope went to the Augustinian general, Gabriel della Volta. He was told to "quiet that man

Luther Meets Cajetan

Again Luther faced great danger. "Now you must die," he told himself as he walked to Augsburg with his friend Leonard Beier. He thought of the disgrace he would bring to his parents if he were burned at the stake. But God's will must be done. "Even at Augsburg, yea, in the midst of His enemies, Jesus Christ rules!" he reasoned.

In October 1518 Luther met three times with Cajetan. The cardinal had orders from Rome not to debate with Luther. Luther was simply to be asked to recant, or take back, what he had said and written. If he did this, he would be forgiven and would again be a "true son of the church." If he did not, other steps would be taken.

Luther was very humble before Cajetan, prostrating himself at the cardinal's feet and asking forgiveness for waiting to appear until the safe-conduct had arrived. At first the cardinal was friendly with him, but they could not agree. Luther would not recant unless someone showed him from the Bible that he was wrong. Cajetan could not do this. He finally became angry and ordered Luther to leave and not return unless he was ready to recant. Vicar Staupitz and Wenceslaus Link, who had come to Augsburg to help Luther, heard a rumor that Cajetan was planning to arrest both Luther and Staupitz. They left Augsburg quickly.

Luther stayed in Augsburg to write two more letters to Cajetan informing him that he would appeal his case directly to Rome. When no reply came, Luther's friends rushed him out of Augsburg during the night of October 20. They escorted him out of the city through a small gate in the city wall and gave him an unmanageable horse on which he rode to Monheim. It was a wild ride that Luther never forgot.

On the trip back to Wittenberg, Luther saw a copy of an announcement by the pope. In it the pope had called Luther a heretic (one who believes or teaches false doctrine); the pope had found him guilty without even hearing his side! Now Luther knew that he could no longer expect fair treatment from Rome. He arrived back in Wittenberg on the afternoon of October 31, 1518, the first anniversary of the posting of the Ninety-five Theses.

Cajetan wrote to Frederick, calling Luther a heretic and asking that he be sent to Rome or forced to leave Saxony. Luther defended himself against Cajetan's charges. He said he would appeal to a general church council.

Frederick was in a tight spot, but he knew how much both the pope and the emperor needed him at that time. He turned to his university professors for advice. Almost all of them were on Luther's side. Frederick wanted to do his Christian duty. If Luther was right, then it would be a sin against God to turn him over to his enemies. If he was wrong, then certainly there were enough learned men in the church to show him his mistakes. This could be done only if Luther were given a fair chance to explain his ideas. He forwarded Cajetan's letter to Luther and asked him to reply to all the charges that had been made. Then he would make a decision about what to do about his most illustrious professor.

The Pope Sends Miltitz

The pope knew he would have to win Frederick's support to silence Luther. His next move was to send a special representative to see Frederick. This man, Karl von Miltitz (1490–1529), was thought to be a wise choice. He was from Saxony and was related to Frederick. He might be able to coax the elector to do what angry orders had failed to do.

Miltitz brought several favors from the pope. One of these was the "Golden Rose," a rose that the pope blessed and gave each year to the Christian ruler who had done the most for the church.

To prepare for the Miltitz visit, the pope wrote letters to many of Frederick's

friends and advisors asking that they try to influence Frederick to "act against Martin and his followers." The Wittenberg faculty wrote a long letter to Frederick supporting Luther; the original letter had been written by Luther himself and edited by members of the faculty.

As he crossed Germany, Miltitz found that many people were on Luther's side. Frederick would not give up Luther, even if it cost him the pope's gifts. So Miltitz became very friendly. He put most of the blame for the trouble on Tetzel.

After talking with Luther, Miltitz promised to speak well of him to the pope. Luther said that he would stop preaching against indulgences if his enemies would stop attacking him. Luther also agreed to have a German bishop examine his teachings and point out any errors in them. The men parted in peace.

Tetzel was made to bear the blame for the trouble. Miltitz was angry with him, and his Dominican friends abandoned indulgence salesman. When Luther heard that Tetzel was alone and friendless, he wrote to him: "Don't take it too hard. You didn't start this trouble. The child has another father." Tetzel died in disgrace on August 11, 1519.

In his report to the pope, Miltitz made it sound as if Luther had taken back all he had said. The pope quickly forgave Luther and welcomed him back to the church. He was eager to end this trouble in Germany, for he had other problems on his mind.

Then, suddenly, Emperor Maximilian died. Church matters were forgotten for a while as a new emperor had to be chosen. God was giving Luther still more time.

Review Questions and Study Projects

1. Underline the correct word or group of words.

   a. Emperor (Maximilian I, Frederick II) believed the false stories he heard about Luther.

   b. In attacking indulgences, Luther was really attacking (the monks, Pope Leo X).

   c. The pope ordered (the police, Cardinal Cajetan) to arrest and hold Luther.

   d. If Luther refused to take back what he had written and said, he would be (excommunicated, put to death) by the church.

   e. God gave Luther a strong protector, (Frederick the Wise of Saxony, Albert of Brandenburg).

   f. The pope and the emperor needed all the help they could get to fight the (Huns, Turks).

   g. Frederick was one of seven princes who (elected, fought) the emperor.

   h. Luther met with Cajetan in (Augsburg, Leipzig) in 1518.

   i. Cajetan wanted Luther to (explain, recant) what he had said.

   j. For teaching as he did, the pope called Luther a (reformer, heretic).

   k. The pope sent (Karl von Miltitz, Albert of Mainz) to get Frederick's help against Luther.

   l. Miltitz blamed (Elector Frederick, John Tetzel) for Germany's religious troubles.

2. Read Matthew 5:11–12. What comfort could Luther take from these words of Christ?

_____

_____

_____

3. God uses rulers and nations to carry out His will. How did events in the lives of these people aid the Reformation?

   a. The Turks:

_____

_____

_____

   b. Frederick the Wise:

_____

_____

_____

c. Emperor Maximilian:

_____

_____

_____

4. a. Why did Luther refuse to recant when Cajetan asked him to?

_____

_____

b. Why was refusing to recant the right thing to do?

_____

_____

5. What does Luther's letter to the dying Tetzel show us about Luther?

_____

_____

6. Imagine you are one of the professors Frederick asked for advice when Cajetan asked him to send Luther to Rome. What would you have told Frederick and why? Write a letter to Frederick giving your advice.

7. Define these words:

recant _____

heretic _____

council _____

representative _____

8. Map work: On the map on page 4 place an H next to Augsburg.

9. Research and present a report on one of the following topics:

Cardinal Cajetan   The Diet of Augsburg

Karl von Miltitz   Emperor Maximilian I

Even though I walk through the valley of the shadow of death, I will fear no evil, for You are with me; Your rod and Your staff, they comfort me (Psalm 23:4).

My Prayer

Dear Lord, thank You for sending people such as Martin Luther and others who were not afraid to stand up for Your Word. Give me Your Spirit that I, too, may be Your faithful witness. I ask this in Jesus' name. Amen.

10 Eck and Excommunication

In his discussions with Miltitz, Luther had agreed to be silent if his opponents would also keep silent. They did not keep the bargain.

Doctor Andreas Karlstadt, a friend of Luther from Wittenberg, wrote a defense of Luther's Ninety-five Theses after the theses had been attacked by Dr. John Eck of Ingolstadt. True to his promise, Luther remained silent while Eck and Karlstadt exchanged letters. Eck, however, kept attacking Luther in his replies to Karlstadt.

Finally Duke George, ruler of the other half of Saxony, invited Eck and Karlstadt to a face-to-face debate at Leipzig. Luther went along, hoping he would have a chance to take part in the debate and defend himself against Eck's charges. In June 1519 Luther rode the 40 miles to Leipzig with several other professors, including Philip Melanchthon, Nicolaus von Amsdorf, and Johann Lang. Two hundred students with spears and battle-axes came along to protect them.

The debate was held at Duke George's Pleissenburg Castle from June 27 to July 16, 1519. According to the rules, one man would rise and speak for half an hour. Then the other would get a turn. Four secretaries wrote down all that was said. These notes would be sent to several universities for judging.

For the first week Eck debated with Karlstadt. Trusting in his great memory, Eck used neither notes nor books. Karlstadt, on the other hand, paged through a pile of books as he spoke. This was very boring for the audience, but Karlstadt's arguments would look strong when the records were later read and judged. Noticing this, Eck asked that the rules be changed so that no books could be used.

Luther and John Eck debated at Leipzig in 1519.

The audience supported the idea. From then on Karlstadt began losing the debate. Karlstadt's clever questioning, however, had already made Eck admit that when compared to grace and God, man's will is simply "a slave and a servant." It was an admission by Eck that Karlstadt's main thesis, that human unregenerated will is powerless to do good works, was correct.

Luther versus Eck

Luther took over for Karlstadt on July 4, 1519. The main point debated by Luther and Eck was, "How and when did the pope become the head of the Christian church?" In an effort to portray Luther as an opponent of papal authority, Eck insisted that Christ Himself had made Peter the first pope. Luther argued that there was no pope until hundreds of years after Christ lived on earth. Eck used the writings of the early church fathers and the laws and decrees of church councils to support his arguments. Luther said, "With all due respect for the fathers, I will rather hold by the Bible."

"Articles of faith can be established only on the basis of Holy Scripture; only there can divine right be found."

By citing Scripture and the early church fathers, Luther emphasized that Christ was the head of the church. When Eck saw that Luther was getting the better of the argument, he compared Luther with Jan Hus. This was a clever move. Hus had been burned as a heretic in 1415, but his followers kept alive his ideas. People in this part of Saxony hated the Hussites because they had often invaded Saxon lands from nearby Bohemia, ruining much property. When Luther replied that some of Hus's ideas were correct, many in the audience turned against him. Duke George shouted, "The plague is upon us!" He became and remained Luther's fierce opponent.

CPH

In *Freedom of the Christian* Luther discussed the freedom that belongs to a Christian who trusts in Jesus for forgiveness. The believer no longer is slave to his own desires. In this writing Luther also pointed out that a Christian willingly serves others out of love for them and for the Lord.

After more discussion of penance, indulgences, and purgatory, the debate came to an end. Eck's followers thought he had won, and after this the pope looked to him as a leader in the fight against false teachings. On the other hand, Luther's friends were just as proud of their champion. He had not backed down before the great John Eck.

This debate made Luther realize how far from the teachings of Rome his own teachings were. For him the Bible was far more important than all the writings of church fathers, decrees of popes or coun-

Luther burned the books of church law to show he would be bound only by the Scriptures. Into the flames he also threw the pope's letter condemning him and his teachings.

cils, and church laws. In the Scriptures it was God, not men, who spoke. Come what may, Luther's conscience was bound by God's holy Word. He was convinced that *sola Scriptura* (Scripture alone) had to be the basis for church doctrine.

If Eck and the church officials thought Luther was finished, they were wrong. Luther and his followers wrote tracts, or pamphlets, to further explain the discussions with Eck. These tracts soon spread all over Germany. The debate with Eck had made Luther a famous man.

Luther Attacks Church Doctrines

In 1520 Luther wrote several important booklets, among them his *Sermon on Good Works* in which he stated that "only those works that God commanded are good; only those works that God has forbidden are sinful. The first and greatest good work is faith in Christ." He said that the pope was not above earthly rulers. He argued that any Christian, if he studied carefully, could understand Scripture as

well as the pope. He complained about the evil lives of many church leaders.

The Roman Catholic Church teaches that there are seven sacraments. Luther stated that there are really only three— Baptism, the Lord's Supper, and Penance— and he was not so sure about Penance. The church taught that the only way to God was through a priest. Luther said that all men are priests and can pray directly to God.

The Roman Church taught that in the Lord's Supper the bread and wine are *changed* into Christ's body and blood by the priest. The priest then "sacrificed" the body and blood of Christ for the people's sins and gave only the bread to the people. In his treatise *On the Babylonian Captivity of the Church* Luther denied this teaching. He showed from the Bible that Jesus' death on the cross paid for all sins for all time and that His body doesn't need to be sacrificed again. The Scriptures also make it clear that in the Sacrament of the Altar the bread and wine remain, but the believer also receives the true body and blood of Jesus. Luther urged that the people be given the wine as well as the bread because this is the way Jesus gave the Lord's Supper to His disciples.

In a book sent to Pope Leo X as a gift, Luther showed how a Christian could be "a free lord, subject to no one," and at the same time be "the servant of all, subject to all." Luther explained that by giving us heaven as a gift, God has freed us from all fear. In thanks to God for this freedom, the Christian joyfully serves others with works of kindness and love.

While Luther was writing, Eck was on his way to Rome. There he reported on the Leipzig Debate. The curia, or church court, then held a special meeting. With the help of Eck and Cajetan, they drew up a list of 41 "errors" made by Luther. A papal bull, or pope's letter, was sent to Luther. It demanded that he take back his "false teachings" within 60 days or face excommunication. (Bull comes from the Latin *bulla*, the word for lead, which was heated and used to seal official documents from popes and emperors.)

If the pope thought this bull would frighten Luther into silence, he was mistaken. Many people were glad that Luther had the courage to point out things that were wrong with the church. Frederick the Wise had made up his mind to protect Luther. Most important, Luther could not help but speak the truth of the Gospel.

Eck had the job of announcing the papal bull in Germany. He found this job very dangerous. The people tore down his posters and threatened him. He was glad to get back to Ingolstadt alive.

Luther Burns the Papal Bull

Some of Luther's enemies burned his books publicly. When Luther heard of it, he, too, had a bonfire. On December 10, 1520, Luther posted an announcement of his own book-burning. Outside the walls of Wittenberg, Luther burned books of church law and the writings of the fathers.

Then, when the fire was roaring hot, he pulled out a small book containing a copy of the papal bull. As he threw it into the flames, he said, "Because you have destroyed the truth of God, may the Lord destroy you in these flames."

Luther's break with the church had finally come.

Review Questions and Study Projects

1. Read each sentence carefully. If the sentence is true, circle the T. If it is false, circle the F.

T   F   a. Luther's friend Dr. Karlstadt defended the Ninety-five Theses against Eck's attacks.

T   F   b. Karlstadt depended on his memory, but Eck used many books while he debated.

T   F   c. Luther and Eck debated on the question of when the pope became the head of the church.

T   F   d. According to Eck, St. Peter was the first pope. Luther said the first pope was St. Paul.

T   F   e. Luther gained support when he said that many of the ideas of Jan Hus were correct.

T　F　f. In the debate, Luther depended mainly on the Bible to support his teachings.

T　F　g. Each man believed he had won the debate.

T　F　h. The debate proved that Luther still believed all that the Roman Catholic Church taught.

T　F　i. After the debate, Luther stopped writing about the church's teachings.

T　F　j. Luther taught that man cannot deal with God without a priest.

T　F　k. Luther believed that the true body and blood of Jesus are received in Holy Communion.

T　F　l. The church warned Luther that he would be excommunicated unless he gave up his beliefs.

T　F　m. Luther was not frightened by the pope's warning.

T　F　n. In burning the papal bull, Luther showed that he would obey God before he would obey any man.

2. Study Acts 4:13–21. Luther was told to stop his preaching and teaching. What did Peter and John answer when they were told the same thing?

_____

_____

_____

_____

_____

3. The church taught that people could go to God only through priests. What does 1 Peter 2:9 say about this?

_____

_____

_____

_____

_____

4. Read the following Bible passages, and check the correct statement of each pair.

a. 1 Corinthians 14:37; 2 Peter 1:21

_____ Christians believe the Bible because it was written very long ago by great men such as Moses, Paul, and Peter.

_____ Christians believe the Bible because, though written by men, it is God's Word.

b. Matthew 7:24–27

_____ A life built on God's Word will last forever.

_____ The average Christian will be safest if he simply believes what he is told.

c. Psalm 119:130

_____ Only well-educated people can understand the Bible.

_____ A common person can understand the way to salvation from the Bible.

d. Acts 17:11

_____ To see whether or not a church teaches correctly, we should ask its pastor.

_____ To see whether or not a church teaches God's truth, we need to compare its teachings to what God's Word teaches.

5. Define these words:

decree _____

curia _____

tracts _____

papal bull _____

ordination _____

6. Map work: On the map on page 4 place an I near Leipzig. This is where Luther and Eck held their great debate. Place a J near Ingolstadt; Eck was a professor at the university there.

7. Eck compared Luther to Jan Hus. Make a report about Hus, explaining what he taught and what happened to him. Other students can make similar reports about Andreas Karlstadt and Erasmus of Rotterdam.

You diligently study the Scriptures because you think that by them you possess eternal life. These are the Scriptures that testify about Me (John 5:39).

My Prayer

Gracious Father in heaven, I cannot thank You enough for Your holy Word, through which I know of Your love for me in Jesus. Help me believe and trust it as long as I live. For Jesus' sake. Amen.

11 The Diet of Worms

In January 1521 the pope declared Luther a heretic and excommunicated him. This meant that he was to be cut off from the church as a dead branch is cut from a tree. His books were to be burned, and his followers were warned to leave him.

Meander, the pope's messenger in Germany, tried to get the new emperor, Charles V, to declare Luther an outlaw. If this were done, he could be hunted and killed like an animal.

Charles was a faithful Roman Catholic. He believed that "a single friar who goes counter to all Christianity for a thousand years must be wrong." He ordered Luther's books to be burned in the Netherlands. He would have done away with Luther at once if it were possible, but in Germany he had to watch his step.

First of all, Charles was not a German. Charles was ruler over Germany only because the electors had chosen him emperor, and one of these electors was Luther's friend Frederick the Wise of Saxony. He also knew that many other Germans supported Luther, including some knights who promised to fight if necessary to protect him. Furthermore, as emperor, Charles had agreed to uphold German laws. These laws included one that said that no German could be outlawed without a fair trial.

Then, too, Charles was worried about the French and the Turks. To be safe against them, Charles needed the help of the German princes. He feared that even the pope could not be trusted, since the pope had tried to keep Charles from being elected emperor.

Charles had many things to think about as he traveled to Worms in January 1521. He was on his way to meet with his first German diet, the council of nobles that made the laws for Germany.

Luther Goes to Worms

Charles summoned Luther to appear before the diet in April of that year. Here Luther would be examined—asked questions—but would not be allowed to argue or explain his teachings. Although Luther's friends advised him not to go to Worms, Luther would not listen to them. He was determined to go. He told them, "Christ still lives, and I shall enter Worms in spite of the gates of hell and the powers of darkness." The emperor then sent a safe-conduct, or letter, promising Luther that he would be safe.

On April 2, 1521, a small group left Wittenberg for Worms, 300 miles to the southwest. Luther and three friends rode in a carriage. Before them rode the brilliantly

Holy Roman Emperor Charles V.

dressed herald of the emperor bearing the imperial banner.

All along the way people came out to see Luther, who was now a hero to many Germans. Here was the man who dared to stand up against both pope and emperor! At Leipzig, Erfurt, and Eisenach old friends wished him well. He preached to large audiences at both the Augustinian monastery at Erfurt and in Eisenach. At the outskirts of Worms, on April 16, 1521, a hundred horsemen met the party. God was giving Luther courage to face his trial.

Luther before the Diet

The next afternoon, April 17, at four o'clock, Luther was led to the bishop's palace, where the emperor and diet were meeting in an upstairs room. He was summoned to appear at about 6 p.m. The room was packed. Spanish and German soldiers lined the walls of the narrow room. On all sides were princes, electors, bishops, and knights. Emperor Charles V was a thin, young man of 20. He was dressed in black, with a large jewel on his chest.

All eyes were on Luther as he entered the room. Everyone knew what lay at the bottom of this meeting. The power of the pope had been challenged. If the pope were to keep his power, Luther must admit he was wrong. "God, be with me!" he prayed in his heart as he faced this mighty group.

An officer warned Luther not to speak except to answer questions. Then the questioner stepped forward. He asked Luther a double question: "Dr. Luther, did you write these books, and are you ready to admit you were wrong in what you wrote?"

Luther was about to answer when his lawyer, Dr. Jerome Schurff, asked that the titles of the books be read. One by one the titles of 25 books that were piled on a small table were read aloud. Having had time to think, Luther answered the first question, "Yes, these books are mine, and I have written others."

To the question about recanting

Luther said, "This question touches God and His Word and the salvation of souls. I beg you, give me time to think it over."

Luther was not stalling. He was not afraid of the emperor, but he realized the seriousness of the question. His answer would be a confession of faith to God Himself. The moment was very much like when he said the Mass for the first time, 14 years earlier, and had trembled before God's majesty.

The emperor gave Luther one day to give his answer.

In the bishop's palace that once stood next to this cathedral in Worms, Luther defended himself in the presence of Emperor Charles V.

"I Will Not Recant"

The next day, April 18, 1521, Luther again faced the diet, which had been moved to a larger room. No longer was he timid or nervous before these great nobles. He thought seriously about his answer. He had prayed most of the night, and God had strengthened him for this test.

When he was again asked, "Do you recant?" his answer was firm and strong. In both Latin and German he pointed out that the books were not all of one kind. Some of them dealt with simple matters of faith and life; even his enemies would find nothing wrong with these. Another group pointed out the evils in the papacy and church government. To recant these would only open the door for more evil. A third group contained attacks on the enemies of the Gospel. If he used strong words in these, it was because he was defending the teachings of Christ with all his might. To reject these would make papal power even stronger. Luther finished by saying that if someone could show him from the Bible that he was wrong, he himself would burn his books.

This answer did not please the emperor. After a brief break for consultation, the questioner asked, "Luther, you have not given a clear answer. Give me a simple yes or no—do you or do you not recant these books?"

Luther's answer was simple and brave. "Unless I am shown my mistakes from the Scriptures or plain reason, I am bound by the Scriptures. My conscience has been taken captive by the Word of God. I am neither able nor willing to recant, since it is neither safe nor right to act against conscience. Here I stand. I can do no other. God help me. Amen." It was the most resounding answer in the history of Christianity.

A great noise broke out as everyone in the room started talking excitedly. The emperor angrily left the room, and the meeting was over.

"Burn the heretic!" muttered the emperor's Spanish friends as Luther left the room. Outside, however, Luther's friends cheered him and shook his hands. With a great sigh Luther raised his arms like a victorious knight and shouted, "I came through! I came through!" Yet Luther was not naïve and was well aware of the consequences of his stand.

Charles wanted to declare Luther an outlaw as soon as his three-week safe period was over, but some members of the diet were afraid this might cause Luther's many followers to revolt. They had all seen the peasant's boot placards around Worms advocating a peasant revolution. They urged Charles to let a committee try once more to change Luther's mind.

This group met with Luther several times. It was no use. Luther insisted that they show him from the Bible where he was wrong. "Convince me from the Scriptures," he said. Then, citing Acts 5:38–39, he continued, "If this plan or this undertaking is of men, it will fail; but if it is of God, you will not be able to overthrow it. You might even be found opposing God."

On April 26 Luther and his three friends left Worms to return to Wittenberg. The night before he had written the emperor, "I have tried to do nothing but reform the church in conformity with the Holy Scriptures." His life might now end at any moment, but Luther had placed himself entirely in the hands of his heavenly Father.

Luther's stand at Worms was a momentous moment in the history of Christianity and Western civilization. For the first time, the principle of freedom of conscience was stated as a right of all humans. Of course, Luther's conscience was shaped by God's Word. Luther had separated himself from the traditional Roman hierarchical system and the method used by the scholastics for interpreting Scripture. By God's grace, he had established the three pillars of the Reformation: grace alone; faith alone; Scripture alone.

Review Questions and Study Projects

1. Tell why Emperor Charles V was not free to deal with Luther as he would have wished.

_____

_____

_____

_____

2. Why did Luther decide to go to Worms?

_____

_____

_____

_____

3. How did God strengthen Luther's courage before he faced the emperor?

_____

_____

_____

_____

4. a. Why didn't Luther immediately answer the second question about recanting his writings?

_____

_____

_____

_____

   b. What can we learn from this?

_____

_____

_____

_____

5. What did Luther mean by this statement: "It is neither safe nor right to act against conscience"?

_____

_____

_____

_____

6. "Convince me from the Scriptures," Luther said to those who wanted him to recant. Why did he insist on this?

_____

_____

_____

_____

7. Describe an occasion when you need to stand up for Jesus.

_____

_____

_____

_____

8. Define these words:

diet _____

herald _____

9. Map work: On the map on page 4 place a K near Worms. To mark Luther's route there, draw a red line from Wittenberg to Worms, passing through Leipzig, Erfurt, and Eisenach.

10. Research and present a report on one of the following topics:

　　Edict of Worms

　　Charles V

　　Ferdinand and Isabella of Spain

　　Emperor Maximilian I

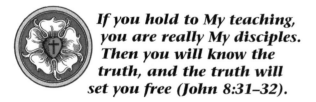

If you hold to My teaching, you are really My disciples. Then you will know the truth, and the truth will set you free (John 8:31–32).

My Prayer

Dear God, help me fear, love, and trust in You above all things. Give me the courage, as You gave Luther, to stand up for Your truth at all times. In Jesus' name I ask it. Amen.

12 In Hiding at the Wartburg

On May 26, 1521, Emperor Charles V signed the Edict of Worms. This order made Luther an outlaw. No one was to have anything to do with him. Every citizen had the duty to seize Luther and turn him over to the authorities. He could be killed on sight.

One month before this edict was issued, Luther had left Worms to return to Wittenberg, but he didn't get there. Frederick the Wise saw to that.

Frederick was sure that the emperor would sign an edict declaring Luther an outlaw. Knowing that Luther's life would be in great danger, the elector made plans to keep him safe. These plans called for Luther to "disappear" until things became quiet again in Germany.

Corbis

The Wartburg castle near Eisenach was Luther's place of refuge during much of 1521.

Luther Is "Kidnapped"

On their way back to Wittenberg Luther and his friends stopped in some of the towns along the way, where Luther preached to large crowds. Since the road led near Moehra, Luther decided to visit his grandmother and his Uncle Heinz.

On May 4, after spending a night with his relatives, Luther and his friends were again in the carriage, bumping along through some heavy woods. When they reached a place near the Castle Altenstein, where the trees were very thick, they heard the drumming of hoofbeats. A group of armed horsemen suddenly burst from the forest and surrounded the carriage. One of Luther's friends, the monk Petzensteiner, leaped from his seat and ran for his life. The driver was sent sprawling under the wagon by a blow from one of the riders. Luther grabbed his Hebrew Bible and his Greek New Testament.

"Which one is Luther?" growled one of the men.

An outdoor service was conducted near Steinbach, Germany, in 1983 at the site where Luther was captured on May 4, 1521.

Corbis

When Luther identified himself, they hurried him into the woods and let Nicolaus Amsdorf and the driver continue their journey.

Once out of sight, his captors gave Luther some knight's clothing and brought him a horse. Then they rode off, taking roundabout trails and hidden pathways so that they would meet few people along the way. Shortly before midnight they arrived at the Wartburg. Here his captors roughly threw Luther into a cell and acted as if he were a dangerous criminal so that the guard would not suspect who he was. This nearly deserted castle just south of Eisenach was to be Luther's hiding place.

The secret of Luther's disappearance was very well kept. Not even Frederick knew exactly where his men had taken Luther. When the news spread through Germany, his friends feared—and his enemies hoped—that he would never return.

Luther as Knight George

To make sure no one would know him, Luther let his hair and beard grow long. He learned knightly manners and took the name Knight George. When his guards thought it was safe, they let him go on walks through the beautiful country-side. Perhaps Luther saw again some scenes that he remembered from his Eisenach school days, more than 20 years earlier.

Once he went along on a hunt. Luther did not enjoy this, for he loved the animals that were hunted. He caught a rabbit and wrapped it in his cloak to save it. After he had left it, the dogs found the rabbit and bit it to death through the cloth. "That is how Satan and the pope would destroy souls and are not stopped by my labor," he said.

From the window of his room high in a tower Luther could see far out over the Thuringian hills. "In the land of the birds," as he called it, he found peace and quiet.

Worry and Work

Yet Luther was not truly happy at the Wartburg. He wanted to be back in Wittenberg preaching, teaching, and wit-nessing for Christ. The reformer also was sick for quite a while after he entered the

Luther's portrait as "Knight George" was painted by Lucas Cranach in 1521.

phlets, and letters. These were taken to a printer, and soon copies were appearing all over Germany. People read them with joy, for this meant that Dr. Luther was still alive.

Luther then began the big job of translating the New Testament from Greek into German. The German language differed in various parts of the country. Luther used a kind of German that could be understood in all parts of Germany. In his work he consulted various Greek and Latin lexicons and dictionaries. It took him only 11 weeks to finish this great task. By September 21, 1522, it was in print. Five thousand copies were sold in only two months. Now many more people could learn to know Jesus by reading Scripture, as Luther himself had done.

Wartburg. His worst troubles, however, were his doubts. Now that he had much time alone, he began to ask himself, "Are you the only one who is wise, Luther? Have all the leaders of the church been wrong for hundreds of years? What if you are wrong? Then you will be leading many people to hell!"

Luther knew that this was Satan tempting him to stop his work of leading people to know Christ. Only through much prayer was he able to fight off the devil's attacks.

Work was Luther's best answer to his worries. To help pastors preach the Gospel clearly, he developed introductions to the Gospel readings and model sermons for each Sunday, Advent through Lent. He completed studies of Psalms 37 and 68 and the Magnificat. He wrote books, pam-

> *The faith that is the right one, rich in grace, demanded by God's word and deed, is that you firmly believe Christ is born for you and that his birth is yours, and come to pass for your benefit. For the Gospel teaches that Christ was born for our sake and that he did everything and suffered all things for our sake, just as the angel says here: "I announce to you a great joy which will come to all people; for to you is born this day a Savior who is Christ the Lord" [Luke 2:10–11]. From these words you see clearly that he was born for us.*
>
> *He does not simply say: "Christ is born," but "for you is he born." Again, he does not say: "I announce a joy," but "to you do I announce a great joy."*

From Martin Luther's sermon for Christmas Eve. Reprinted from *Luther's Works,* American Edition, vol. 52, edited by Hans J. Hillerbrand, copyright © 1974 Fortress Press, pages 14–15. Used by permission of Augsburg Fortress.

Luther's study at the Wartburg.

Troubles at Home

Meanwhile Luther was receiving letters from some people in Wittenberg who knew where he was. These letters began to worry him. Dr. Karlstadt and Gabriel Zwilling were acting as leaders while Luther was away. These men believed in Luther's ideas, but they pushed ahead too fast with changes in the churches at Wittenberg.

Statues and images were taken out and burned. Priests, monks, and nuns were told that they must marry. German was used in the worship service instead of Latin. People were forced to take both bread and wine at Holy Communion. Karlstadt wore no vestments when he conducted a Christmas Eve Mass. Altars, candles, crucifixes, and even church music were no longer used in church services. Parishioners in Wittenberg heatedly debated all these developments.

To add to the confusion, three men from Zwickau came to Wittenberg in December 1521, claiming to be prophets of the Lord. "The Bible is not important," they said, "since God speaks to us directly." The Zwickau "prophets" spoke against the baptizing of children, since only adults, they said, could understand Baptism's real meaning.

Luther's friend Philip Melanchthon was so upset by all this that he was ready to leave the university. Frederick the Wise also was troubled. Mobs were running wild in Wittenberg, and he feared the riots might spread to other towns.

Luther Returns to Wittenberg

Finally the town council of Wittenberg, against Frederick's will, sent Luther a letter begging him to return. Luther immediately accepted and left the Wartburg. In March 1522 he reached Wittenberg and began to set things straight.

Back in his own pulpit, Luther preached a series of powerful sermons to his people. He urged the people of Wittenberg to be patient, to let God's Word work on people's hearts. "When we have won men's hearts, the evils will die out by themselves. We must never use force. The whole life of a Christian is faith and love," he told his hearers.

In a very short time order was restored to Wittenberg. Luther was back to stay. Many problems remained to be solved, and new ones would arise. God had much work for His servant Luther.

Review Questions and Study Projects

1. Fill in the blanks below with words from the story.

When _____ signed the _____, Luther was declared an _____. Since this meant that he could be _____ by anyone, his ruler, _____, had him "kidnapped" and taken to the _____ castle near _____ for safekeeping.

While he was there, Luther was known as _____. He let his hair and _____ grow and even went along on a _____ with the other knights, although he didn't care much for it. His main work while there was the translation of the _____ into _____.

Letters came to Luther telling him that things were not going well in _____. _____ and Zwilling and the _____ "prophets" were making _____ in the church so fast that people were confused and upset. The town _____ wrote Luther asking him to return and to put things in order again. Luther did so by preaching strong _____ in which he begged the people to let _____ _____ work the changes in people's hearts.

2. Read the second and third sections of the narrative again; list at least three things that were done to make Luther's kidnapping seem real and to keep his hiding place a secret.

_____

_____

_____

_____

3. The devil often uses doubt to tempt God's children. Read Matthew 4:1–11, and tell how we can fight Satan's attacks.

_____

_____

_____

_____

_____

4. Explain what Luther meant when he said, "When we have won men's hearts, the evils will die out by themselves."

_____

_____

_____

_____

5. When Luther was forced to stay at the Wartburg, he used the time to write books and even to translate the New Testament. How can we make good use of our time when we are sick or hurt and have to stay at home?

_____

_____

_____

_____

_____

_____

_____

_____

6. Define these words: edict   crucifix

7. Map work: On the map on page 4 find Eisenach. Just a little below it place a dot and print Wartburg. Here Luther stayed from May 1521 to March 1522. Label Zwickau with an L and Moehra with an M.

8. In *Luther's Works* find one of Luther's sermons. Summarize a portion of it for your class. Write a prayer to accompany your summary.

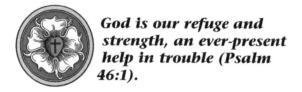 *God is our refuge and strength, an ever-present help in trouble (Psalm 46:1).*

My Prayer

Dear Father in heaven, with Your mighty power protect me from all danger. Give me the strength to resist the devil's temptations. Keep me always as Your own dear child. I ask these things for the sake of Jesus, my Savior. Amen.

13 Beginnings of the Lutheran Church

Martin Luther never intended to start a new church. His study of the Bible convinced him that many of the teachings of the church in his day were man-made. Luther wanted the church to stop teaching these errors and return to the pure doctrine taught by Christ and His apostles.

The leaders of the church, however, felt that the church could never go wrong. They concluded that Luther must be a false teacher, and they would not listen to him. His enemies spread lies about him. The pope excommunicated him. In the Edict of Worms the Holy Roman Emperor declared that he was an outlaw and should be hunted as one. Although Luther did not want it to be this way, he was now out of the Church of Rome.

Many people believed that God spoke powerfully through Martin Luther. They risked punishment to read his writings and hear his sermons. Much of northern Germany looked to him for leadership. Luther's sense of duty and devotion to the truths of God's Word would not allow him simply to ignore these people and send them back to their old ways of worship. A new church had to be built. Despite Luther's objections, people called the new church the "Lutheran" church.

A Bible Church

The cornerstone of this new church was the Bible. To Cajetan, Miltitz, and Eck, Luther had said, "Convince me by Scripture." At the Diet of Worms he had stood firm: "My conscience is bound by the Word of God." To Luther, then, God's Word was the highest authority—higher than the decrees of councils or popes, tra-

Lutheran Film Associates

Luther's translation of the New Testament into German provided a model for those using the language for centuries to come.

ditions, or the writings of the church fathers. Furthermore, Luther believed that God can and does speak directly to human hearts through the Scriptures.

Luther reasoned that if the Christian church is to be built by God's Word working in the hearts and lives of people, they need Bibles in their own language. He had translated the New Testament into German while at the Wartburg in 1521. After his return to Wittenberg, he refined his work; it appeared in print in September 1522. With the help of Hebrew scholars at the University of Wittenberg, he translated the Old Testament, issuing various sections as they were completed. After thorough checking, the entire German Bible appeared in 1534.

Although the price of Luther's completed German Bible was equal to about $20, people eagerly bought it. Over a million copies were sold in the next dozen years.

The Lutheran Catechisms

In 1528 Luther visited the growing number of Lutheran churches in Saxony. He found that things were not going well. Everywhere there were different forms of worship and church practice. Many people, including many pastors, knew little about Christian doctrine. Some could not even recite the Lord's Prayer or the Ten Commandments. To guide them, these new churches needed a clear and simple statement of the teachings of the Bible.

Luther met this need in 1529 by writing two catechisms. He wrote the Large Catechism for pastors and adults. Pastors read parts of it to their congregations and used it to prepare sermons. Luther himself preached sermons based on the catechisms.

Title page of Luther's Small Catechism.

Der kleine Catechifmus für die gemeine Pfar; herr vnd pre; diger. Mart. Luther. Wittemberg.

CPH

Luther wrote the Small Catechism especially for children. In it he explained what is known as the Six Chief Parts of Christian doctrine in clear and simple language. He succeeded remarkably well. For example, it is hard to find a more beautiful confession of faith than his explanation of the Second Article of the Apostles' Creed.

Although the catechisms originally were written to help instruct people in the Christian faith, they also have been included in Lutheranism's Book of Concord as theological and confessional statements of the church. Luther thought the catechisms should be one's "spiritual companion" on the journey from the cradle to the grave because through a study of the catechism the Christian would be helped to put on the mind of Christ, to develop Christlike patterns of thought and life.

> *I believe that Jesus Christ, true God, begotten of the Father from eternity, and also true man, born of the Virgin Mary, is my Lord, who has redeemed me, a lost and condemned person, purchased and won me from all sins, from death, and from the power of the devil; not with gold or silver, but with His holy, precious blood and with His innocent suffering and death, that I may be His own and live under Him in His kingdom and serve Him in everlasting righteousness, innocence, and blessedness, just as He is risen from the dead, lives and reigns to all eternity. This is most certainly true.*

Luther's explanation of the Second Article of the Apostles' Creed, Luther's Small Catechism (St. Louis: Concordia, 1986).

The Lutheran Service

The Mass had to be changed to reflect the new biblical teaching. Those parts of the Mass that made worship an effort to acquire merits for the sinner were eliminated. The doctrine of justification by faith meant that any reference in the mass to sacrificing Christ again had to be removed. People received both bread and wine in the Lord's Supper as was done in the early church.

German replaced Latin as the language used in the service. Explaining God's Word in a sermon became an important part of the service, as did the serving of the Lord's Supper. To Luther the preaching of the Word was the central part of any church service. He himself was a great preacher. "Everyone who hears him once, desires to hear him again and again," wrote one young man after hearing a Luther sermon. Under his direction, the focus of the church service again became Christ's redemptive work.

Because the Bible teaches that each believer is a priest, people were given a more active part in the service. Before this, people only watched and listened to the priests and choirs; now they were invited to sing hymns in their own language. Luther's first German hymnbook appeared in 1524. Luther himself wrote some of the hymns, both words and music. Others were based on older Latin hymns. "Music is second only to the study of God's Word," Luther said. Luther wrote several hymns based on the Six Chief Parts of the Small Catechism to teach the doctrines of the Bible to people. These include "We All Believe in One True God" (*LW* 213), based on the Apostles' Creed, and "Here Is the Tenfold Sure Command" (*LW* 331), based on the Ten Commandments. He also wrote hymns for major parts of the church service. Two of Luther's best-known hymns are "A Mighty Fortress Is Our God" (*LW* 297, 298) and the Christmas hymn "From Heaven Above to Earth I Come" (*LW* 37) and its counterpart, "Welcome to Earth, O Noble Guest" (*LW* 38). Luther also fitted the Gregorian music of the liturgy to German words so that people could understand the church service. Soon the Lutheran church became known as "the singing church" because in it music served the Gospel and enabled the people to participate in worship.

Luther and Education

Luther was also a champion of education. He saw that if the church was to keep growing, more and better schools were needed. In letters to leaders throughout Germany and in Norway and Denmark he urged that good schools be established and maintained. He provided the original rationale for tax-supported public education. He urged parents to send their daughters as well as their sons to school. Here children could be trained to be God-fearing citizens and church members. Luther viewed the school as the partner of the church and the home in teaching God's Word.

For the Lutheran Christian, Luther outlined a whole new way of living. No longer was the life of a monk or nun thought to be the most God-pleasing vocation. The honest labor of every Christian was sacred because God blessed it. No longer were good works done to win God's favor. God gives His favor freely, and the believer does good works because he is a new creature in Christ who loves God and wants to please Him.

No longer was the monastery the chief training ground for Christian living. The Christian home took its place. God surely dwelt in a home where Bible reading and instruction, worship, and prayer were practiced.

To educate adults, Luther advocated that churches and towns sponsor evening lectures. To ensure that education was available to all, he advocated that towns provide money to educate students from poor families. As a result of the improvements in education made during the Reformation, informed clergy and laity were better able to provide leadership for strong congregations and communities, and the lot of the common person was greatly improved.

Review Questions and Study Projects

1. Read the description in Column B, and match it with the answer in Column A by writing the number of the correct answer in the blank.

Column A

1. Schools
2. Lutherans
3. Roman Catholic
4. Six Chief Parts
5. Sermon
6. Christian doctrine
7. German Bible
8. Hymnbook
9. Christian home
10. Small Catechism
11. God's Word
12. Large Catechism

Column B

_____ a. The church from which Luther was excommunicated

_____ b. What Luther's followers came to be called

_____ c. Luther's church was based on this

_____ d. Put God's Word in their everyday language

_____ e. The teachings of a Christian church

_____ f. Book Luther wrote for pastors and adults, containing the main teachings of the Bible

_____ g. Children learn basic Christian teaching from it

_____ h. The main parts of the Small Catechism

_____ i. This helped the Lutheran church become the "singing church"

_____ j. The part of a Lutheran church service in which God's Word is explained

_____ k. Helped church and home in the instruction of children

_____ l. Replaced the monastery as chief training ground for the Christian life

2. Check the line that best completes the following sentences.

a. Luther disagreed with many teachings of the Church of Rome because

_____ (1) his own reason told him they could not be true.

_____ (2) they did not agree with what the Bible teaches.

b. When Luther said, "My conscience is bound by the Word of God," he meant that

_____ (1) he would believe and teach only the truths of the Bible.

_____ (2) the church alone could explain God's Word to sinful men.

c. In the Bible

_____ (1) God speaks directly to people.

_____ (2) God speaks in language that few people can understand.

d. If God's Word is to reach many people

    _____ (1) God must speak to them as He did to Moses and the prophets.

    _____ (2) the people must have Bibles that they can read.

e. Many Bibles were sold in Germany because

    _____ (1) the people were eager to study and learn God's Word.

    _____ (2) the price was very low.

    _____ (3) the church ordered each member to buy one.

f. When Luther visited the new churches of Saxony he found that

    _____ (1) all of them taught and worshiped alike.

    _____ (2) many of them were confused in their teachings and worship.

    _____ (3) they fully understood Christian doctrine.

g. In Holy Communion as celebrated in the Lutheran church

    _____ (1) the pastor drinks the wine while the people receive only the bread.

    _____ (2) the people receive both bread and wine.

h. For his hymnbook Luther

    _____ (1) wrote only the words to the hymns.

    _____ (2) wrote both words and music for some hymns.

    _____ (3) composed only the music for the hymns.

i. Luther was a great preacher, for he preached

    _____ (1) about Jesus and His love for us.

    _____ (2) about Mary, the saints, and great popes.

j. Luther urged parents to send their children to school. He meant

    _____ (1) only boys should be sent.

    _____ (2) both girls and boys should be sent.

k. A new way of life opened for Lutheran Christians because Luther showed them that

    _____ (1) God's richest blessings come to those who live in monasteries.

    _____ (2) their good works earn God's love and favor.

    _____ (3) God blesses all work that is done to His glory.

3. List the Six Chief Parts of Christian doctrine as found in Luther's Small Catechism.

_____

_____

_____

4. Luther wrote many hymns besides those mentioned in the lesson. Use the hymnal's index of authors (*LW*, p. 985), and find another hymn written by Luther. Then write a devotion based on the hymn you select.

5. Write a reply to this question: "Why did Luther break away from the Roman Catholic Church?"

_____

_____

_____

6. a. What were the main changes Luther made in the church service? Why did he make these changes?

_____

_____

_____

b. How did his attitude regarding changes in the church service differ from that of men such as Karlstadt and Zwilling?

_____

_____

_____

7. Define these words:

authority _____

scholars _____

tradition _____

creed _____

interpreter _____

catechism _____

8. Research and make a presentation on one of these topics:

How I might use the catechism throughout my life
Luther's use of hymns in the church service
My favorite Martin Luther hymn
The school day in Luther's time

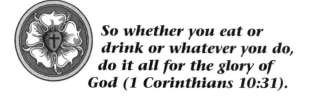

So whether you eat or drink or whatever you do, do it all for the glory of God (1 Corinthians 10:31).

My Prayer

Thank You, dear Lord, for giving me Your precious Word. Through Your Holy Spirit let this Word assure me of forgiveness in Jesus and strengthen me to serve You and others with gladness. Amen.

14 The Luther Home

Should priests and nuns get married? Luther could see no reason why not. Since he believed the home to be a much better training ground for the Christian life than the monastery, he felt that the Roman Church was wrong in forbidding priests, monks, and nuns to marry.

Luther saw that many people wrongly looked upon celibacy (remaining unmarried) as another "good work" by which they tried to please God. Quite a few churchmen broke their vows—and the Sixth Commandment—by living with women without being married to them. Besides, had not God Himself instituted and blessed marriage? Luther's spoken and written attacks on this church rule were so strong that many monks and nuns left their monasteries and married. On October 9, 1524, Luther himself renounced his monastic vows, including the vow of celibacy.

Luther had no desire to be married. "They will never force a wife upon me," he had said at Wittenberg in 1521. His reason was simple: As a heretic and an outlaw, his life was in constant danger.

Several things happened to change his mind, however. In April 1523 a group of 12 nuns escaped, with Luther's help, from a cloister in Marienthron. He asked Leonhard Koppe, a Torgau businessman, to take the nuns out of the convent in a covered wagon that was used to deliver supplies there, including herring in barrels. Evidently Koppe snuck the nuns out of the cloister in his covered wagon on Easter Eve. Three of the nuns returned to their homes, but nine had no place to go, so they were brought to Wittenberg. Luther felt it his duty to find homes, husbands, or jobs for them.

Martin Luther's wedding portrait was painted by Lucas Cranach in 1525.

Katharina von Bora as painted by Lucas Cranach in 1526.

Luther Marries Katharina

After two years, only Katharina von Bora remained unmarried. Katie was a sensible, hard-working young woman. By 1525 she was 26 years old and almost past the marrying age for those times. Two attempts to find a husband for her had failed. She had fallen in love with Jerome Baumgaertner, the son of a distinguished family from Nuremberg, but his family objected to him marrying a runaway nun. After Luther tried to make several other matches for Katie, she said, "I will marry no one but Dr. Amsdorf or Dr. Luther himself." Luther laughed when he heard this.

Yet, as he thought about it more, there were good reasons for him to marry Katie. If he did so, it would strengthen his teaching that marriage is pleasing to God, even for priests. It would certainly please his father, who wanted a grandson to carry on the Luther name. And it would help him too, for he needed someone to look after his everyday needs.

On June 13, 1525, Martin Luther married Katharina von Bora. Their love for each other grew during the nearly 21 years God gave them together as husband and wife.

Family Joys and Sorrows

Martin and Katie Luther made their home in the Black Cloister, which Elector John had given them in 1532. Katie soon showed that she was a good wife. She saw to it that her husband ate and slept regularly and had clean clothes to wear. She ran the house on his small salary.

Katie was a conscientious mother, a hard-working housekeeper, and a manager of farms and gardens. The Luthers maintained four gardens. With money she had saved and a gift from the elector, she bought her family's farm near Zulsdorf from her brother. Katie managed the care of cows, pigs, goats, chickens, geese, doves, and the family dog, Tolpel. She learned to brew beer. Her days were busy with cooking and tending their home.

God blessed this marriage with six children: Johannes, nicknamed Hans after his grandfather; Elizabeth; Magdalena; Martin; Paul; and Margaret. The children

The Luther family singing. Painting by Gustav Adolph Spongenberg (1828–1891).

added much joy to the big house. Luther greatly enjoyed being with them and watching them at play. He never returned from a trip without bringing something along for his children.

Sometimes there was sorrow. Their first daughter, Elizabeth, died before she was a year old. The second daughter, Magdalena, became very sick when she was 13. As death came near, Luther prayed, "Lord, I love her so, but Your will be done."

Kneeling at her bedside, he said to his daughter, "Magdalena, my little girl, you would like to stay with your father here, but are you also willing to go to your Father in heaven?" Smiling weakly, she answered, "Yes, dear father, as God wills."

Magdalene died in her father's arms. When they buried her, Luther wept: "My dear little Lena, how happy you are! You will rise again and shine as the stars, yes, as the sun. . . . It is very strange—to know that she is in peace and well off and yet to be so sad!"

Luther led his family and any guests who happened to be with them in daily devotions. And there was always music in the house. Luther could play the lute and fife, and he had a fine tenor singing voice. He liked to play chess, work in his garden, or work at his lathe. He even mended his own pants.

The doors of the Luther home were open to all. At times, as many as 25 people stayed there. By his nature, Luther could not refuse help to persons in need. He gave what little money he had to poor students or friends. One by one he gave away the gold and silver dishes he and Katie had received as wedding gifts. Katie scolded him, "Are you going to give everything away?" He replied, "God is rich. He will give us more."

Review Questions and Study Projects

1. If the sentence is true, circle the T. If it is false, circle the F.

T   F   a. Remaining unmarried to earn salvation is a God-pleasing good work.

T   F   b. Luther helped some nuns escape from their cloister and found homes for many of them.

T   F   c. Luther and Katharina von Bora fell in love the first time they saw each other.

T   F   d. Luther broke with his church and Katharina left the cloister so they could marry.

T   F   e. God blessed the Luthers with six children.

T   F   f. Two of the Luther children died while still quite young.

T   F   g. Luther carefully saved what little money and property he had for his own family's use.

T   F   h. Even though the Luther family was large, there was always room for guests in the Black Cloister.

2. Luther urged priests, monks, and nuns to marry. Read 1 Timothy 3:1–5 and tell what the Bible says about the marriage of pastors.

_____

_____

_____

3. a. Tell why Luther himself did not get married earlier than he did.

_____

_____

_____

b. Why did he change his mind?

_____

_____

_____

4. Study Ephesians 5:25–33. Describe how husbands are to treat their wives, as God directs in this passage.

_____

_____

_____

5. a. What command does Jesus give in Matthew 5:42?

_____

_____

_____

b. How did Luther obey this Word of God?

_____

_____

_____

6. Imagine that you are a visitor in the Luther home. Write a letter to a friend telling what a typical day is like.

7. Define these words: celibacy   lute   fife

8. Just five people were invited to Martin and Katie's wedding. Research and report on one of these people present: Lucas Cranach, Justus Jonas, Pastor Johannes Bugenhagen.

"For this reason a man will leave his father and mother and be united to his wife, and the two will become one flesh." So they are no longer two, but one. Therefore what God has joined together, let man not separate (Mark 10:7–9).

My Prayer

How can I thank You enough, dear Lord, for Your goodness to me? Help me love, serve, honor, and obey my parents at all times, remembering that they serve in Your place on earth. Guard and keep everyone in our family safe, always trusting in Jesus, so that we may have a long and happy life together. I ask this for Jesus' sake. Amen.

15 More Battles

Against Frederick the Wise's wishes, Luther left the Wartburg to deal with problems at Wittenberg. This local unrest was part of much bigger troubles breaking out all over Germany.

Most of the people in Germany at this time were peasants, or farmers. Very few owned their own land. Even the "common lands," which all the peasants used together, were taken over by the nobles. Taxes were going up, and so were prices. Disease and hunger were common. Peasants found it harder and harder to feed and clothe their families. If they were caught trying to get extra food or fuel from the nobles' forests, they could be put to death. Life for most of them was almost like slavery.

The German peasants had tried to revolt many times. The most recent attempt had been in 1514. Each time the rulers put down the revolt. When the peasants heard about Luther's dispute with the pope, the church, and the imperial diet, they began to ask themselves, "If this one monk can stand up against both church and state, why can't we?"

When Luther wrote and spoke of the "freedom of the Christian," he was talking about man's relation to God. The peasants took it to mean that they were free to change their laws and living conditions and free themselves from the bondage of feudalism.

Luther had spoken against greedy princes and churchmen (the church

CPH

In this woodcut, Christ is inviting His lambs, the peasants, to enter the sheepfold. Where is Christ pictured? Who are the people having the hardest time getting into the sheepfold? Why would this cartoon give peasants courage to rebel against their lords?

owned much property at this time) and had warned them of troubles ahead. But Luther did not want the peasants to use violence to bring about social reforms. He believed that the free preaching of the Gospel would change the hearts of people. When people believed the Gospel, he was sure they would no longer cheat, beat, mistreat, or enslave their fellow Christians or anyone else. Luther told the peasants to suffer quietly rather than use force to make changes.

The Peasants' Revolt (1524–1525)

In spite of all his efforts, a revolt broke out in June 1524. It began in southwestern Germany when the Countess of Lufen tried to force her peasants to pick strawberries for a banquet; they rebelled. Soon the rebellion spread over much of Germany and Austria. The peasants drew up a list of their demands and gave it to the rulers. These demands were known as *The Twelve Articles*. Luther thought that the Articles were fair and the rulers should agree to them. He again warned the peasants not to take the law into their own hands. At the same time he scolded the rulers for their bad treatment of the peasants. "Don't use the Gospel and Christian freedom to justify violence," he told them. "Negotiate."

There had been little bloodshed so far. Now a few troublemakers got busy. Thomas Müntzer told the peasants of Saxony not to listen to Luther. He urged them to destroy the nobles' property and to kill the wicked princes and priests. He wanted to establish God's kingdom by using force to destroy godless people. Other leaders did the same, and soon all of Germany was ablaze with revolt. Over 40 monasteries and castles were destroyed in central Germany alone. In the midst of all this activity, Luther's one sure protector, Elector Frederick the Wise, died on May 5, 1525.

When Luther heard of all this mob action, he was very angry with the rebels. He became incensed when he found out they were using his writings to justify their actions. When he visited the area around Eisleben to help start a Christian school, he saw the damage that had been done. He was heckled during a sermon by those who disagreed with his advice to settle matters peacefully. When he arrived back in Wittenberg, he wrote a tract, *Against the Murderous and Thieving Hordes of Peasants,* in which he called on the rulers to strike down the mobs of peasants without mercy. It was written in anger and contained viciously bitter words. Luther received much justifiable criticism for this tract. To make matters worse, the tract appeared after the peasants had been defeated, making it look as though Luther had taken a position favoring the winning side.

Meanwhile the rulers and princes had gathered regular soldiers and marched into battle against the mobs of farmers. One after another the peasant armies were beaten, and their leaders were killed. A peasant army was crushed in the Battle of Frankenhausen on May 15, 1525. Thomas Müntzer was found hiding in a bed; he was tried for leading rebellion and was executed. By 1526 the revolt of the peasants had been crushed.

When the peasants learned that Luther had called them "thieves" and "murderers" and had called for their destruction, many would have nothing more to do with him. Luther, too, had a change of heart. He tried to explain his position in *An Open Letter to the Peasants,* but he did not apologize for what he had said. He still did not approve of rebellion, especially when God's Word was used to justify rebelling. From this time on, he looked to the princes and nobles to take the lead in the new churches.

The First Diet of Speyer (1526)

The new churches were getting a good start. Emperor Charles V was away fighting his greatest enemy, France, but the German princes went on holding their diets. They talked about the "Lutheran problem" but could not agree on what to do about it. The enemies of Luther wanted to enforce the Edict of Worms, but his many friends would not hear of this. So for five years after the Diet of Worms nothing was done. Luther went on preaching and teaching in Wittenberg under the protection of the elector of Saxony.

Some of the Catholic princes decided to band together to wipe out Lutheranism.

When the Lutheran princes of Germany heard of this, they formed the League of Torgau. They agreed to fight rather than give up their new faith. Now all of Germany was split into two camps, Lutheran and Catholic.

When the diet met in Speyer in 1526, the Catholics and the Lutherans made an important agreement. They agreed to let each prince control church affairs in his own state as he saw fit. This meant that Catholic princes would allow only the Catholic religion, and Lutheran princes would support Luther's new church. Emperor Charles didn't like this, but he could do little about it until he finished his wars with France.

The Second Diet of Speyer (1529)

Three more years went by, and the Lutherans kept growing stronger. In 1529 the second Diet of Speyer made another important decision. In Lutheran states, Catholics as well as Lutherans were to be allowed freedom of worship, but in Catholic states only Catholics would have this freedom.

Of course, the Lutheran princes called this rule unfair. "We protest before God and before men that we will not agree with anything that goes against God's Word," they said in their official statement. From this protest they were called "Protestants," a name still used by many Christians who do not agree with the teachings of the Roman Catholic faith.

Luther and Islam

During the time of the Reformation, followers of Islam (who were called Turks or Mohammadans) became a major threat to Christianity in Europe. The Turks had captured Constantinople in 1453, 30 years before Luther was born. In the next 10 years they took over Bosnia, Serbia, and Herzegovina. When Suleiman I, who was called the Magnificent, became leader of the Turks in 1520, it became obvious that the goal of the Turks was to rule Europe. By 1529 the Turks threatened Vienna, Austria. The major concern of Emperor Charles V was to defend the empire from this threat. He needed both Catholic and Protestant princes to be united in their efforts to

Ulrich Zwingli (1484–1531) believed people received only the bread and wine in Holy Communion. They were symbols of Christ's suffering and death. For him, Christ's body was in heaven, so it could not be in the Sacrament.

Corbis

79

defeat the Turks. For this reason, he attempted to have them settle their religious differences.

After studying the Qur'an, Luther was convinced that Muhammad's teachings were false. The Qur'an, he said, is stuffed "together in confusion from the Law and the Gospel" (*What Luther Says*, §3022). Muhammad "denies that Christ is the Son of God, denies that He died for our sins, denies that He rose again to bring us to life, denies that through faith in Him sins are forgiven and we are justified, denies that He will come as the Judge of the living and the dead — though he does believe in a resurrection of the dead and a day of judgment — denies the Holy Spirit, and denies His gifts" (*What Luther Says*, §3025). Holy Scripture makes it clear that Jesus is God when St. Paul refers to "Christ, who is God over all" (Romans 9:5) and when John says Jesus "is the true God" (1 John 5:20). Yet Islam places Muhammad above Christ. Luther's primary objection to Islam was that it denied that people are justified by faith in Jesus Christ as their Savior.

Nevertheless, Luther supported publishing the Qur'an and making it widely available for Christians to study. He encouraged the city council of Basel to do just that in a letter he wrote to them on October 24, 1542. By reading the Qur'an, Luther wanted Christians to see that the Qur'an did not contain the message of salvation through Jesus. He was interested in refuting Islam, not promoting it.

Luther admired the "courageous, strict, and respectable conduct" of many Islamic people. "They do not indulge in wine, do not over-indulge in drinking and eating as we do, do not dress so frivolously and lavishly. They do not build with our splendor, nor do they put on the airs we do; and they do not curse and swear so much. Toward their emperor and lord they show great ... obedience, decorum, and honor. Moreover, they have organized their government and administer it as we should like to have it administered in German

lands" (*What Luther Says*, §3029). For Luther, Islamic people should be treated with respect for the virtuous lives that they lived. He fervently hoped that they, too, would come to believe the Gospel.

Luther supported the emperor's efforts to defend the empire against any Turkish invasion. While at times he felt that the Turkish threat was God's punishment on the Christian princes for neglecting Word and Sacrament and living evil lives, he urged the Protestant princes to help Charles in his battles with the Turks. He urged people to pay the tax to support the resistance effort and said that if he were not too old and weak, he would prefer personally to be part of the army. His concern, however, was for the spiritual life of the people. He told pastors to urge people to confess their sins and live in response to the Gospel. He told soldiers to pray faithfully, hear the Word, and receive the Sacrament. He encouraged children to learn the catechism. For Luther, growing in the faith as the Holy Spirit works through Word and Sacrament was the best way to resist Islam.

The Sacramentarian Controversy and the Marburg Colloquy (1529)

Luther had been thinking about questions concerning the Lord's Supper for several years. Already in 1519 Karlstadt's ideas about understanding the Words of Institution symbolically had moved Luther to preach a sermon on the subject. Several others had asked Luther about the Lord's Supper, and Luther had always made the point that the bread and wine truly were Christ's body and blood. Late in 1524 Luther answered a letter from reform-minded pastors in Strasbourg, France, asking for his opinion about their idea that the bread and the wine were *symbols* of Christ's body and blood. Their views were close to those of Ulrich Zwingli of Zurich, Switzerland. They followed Erasmus in their humanistic approach to interpreting Scripture; in their view, any Bible passage not clear to human reason should be interpreted in a way that harmonized with reason.

In a sharply worded response, Luther said that human reason could not be allowed to change the plain meaning of Scripture. "This is My body" and "This is My blood" meant just that, even though human reason could not understand how this could be. *Sola Scriptura* permitted no other approach to biblical interpretation.

> *The Word says first of all that Christ has a body, and this I believe. Secondly, that this same body rose to heaven and sits at the right hand of God; this too I believe. It says further that this same body is in the Lord's Supper and is given to us to eat. Likewise I believe this, for my Lord Jesus Christ can easily do what he wishes, and that he wishes to do this is attested by his own words.*

Martin Luther, as quoted in James M. Kittelson, *Luther the Reformer: The Story of the Man and His Career* (Minneapolis: Augsburg, 1986), p. 207.

In 1529 Luther and several of his followers meet with Ulrich Zwingli and his followers at Marburg. Zwingli was attempting to reform the churches in Switzerland, much as Luther was doing in Germany. Philip of Hesse, a Lutheran prince, thought it best if all reform groups would join forces. He arranged the meeting in Marburg, hoping the men could agree in all the important matters.

Luther and Zwingli did agree on many points, as expressed in the *Marburg Articles,* but they disagreed on one very important doctrine—the Lord's Supper. Luther insisted that Christ's body and blood are truly present in the Sacrament. Zwingli said that the bread and wine only *stand* for Christ's body and blood and that Christ is present only in a spiritual way.

Again Luther showed that he was bound by Holy Scripture. The words "This is my body" were enough for him. He accepted them by faith, even though he could not understand how they were true. For Luther, Zwingli had committed the deadly sin of theology when he placed works above grace and reason above obedience to the Holy Scripture. Luther beautifully stated the benefits of the Sacrament in the Small Catechism, which he completed in 1529, the same year as the Marburg Colloquy.

Luther and Zwingli parted without joining forces.

Review Questions and Study Projects

1. a. Why were the German peasants unhappy in Luther's time?

_____

_____

_____

   b. Explain what Luther believed would cause the situation to change.

_____

_____

_____

2. a. Before the Peasants' Revolt, what did Luther tell the rulers?

_____

_____

_____

b. What did Luther tell the peasants?

_____

_____

_____

c. During the revolt, what was Luther's attitude toward the peasants?

_____

_____

_____

d. Explain Luther's "change of heart."

_____

_____

_____

3. Why was the Edict of Worms not enforced and Luther thrown into prison?

_____

_____

_____

4. a. What agreement was reached at the first Diet of Speyer?

_____

_____

_____

b. How was this changed at the second Diet of Speyer?

_____

_____

_____

c. How did the "Protestants" get their name?

_____

_____

_____

5. What was Luther's main objection to Islam?

_____

_____

_____

6. a. What was the purpose of the meeting at Marburg?

_____

_____

b. On what point did Luther and Zwingli disagree?

_____

_____

7. The following three descriptions characterize the teaching of the Catholic, Lutheran, and Reformed churches in regard to the Lord's Supper. Write the name of the church before the statement that describes its teaching.

_____ Bread and wine are not present, only body and blood.

_____ Body and blood are not present, only bread and wine.

_____ Bread and wine and body and blood are actually present.

8. Define these words: peasant league   colloquy

9. Map work: On the map on page 4 indicate Speyer with an N, Torgau with an O, and Marburg with a P.

10. Research one of the following topics and write a short report to present to your class.

Ulrich Zwingli   The Sacramentarian Controversy
Peasants' War   The Marburg Colloquy

Everyone must submit himself to the governing authorities, for there is no authority except that which God has established. The authorities that exist have been established by God. Consequently, he who rebels against the authority is rebelling against what God has instituted (Romans 13:1–2).

My Prayer

I thank You, Father in heaven, for the blessings of Your church. By Your Holy Spirit keep it faithful to Your will and Word. I ask this for Christ's sake. Amen.

16 The Augsburg Confession

Corbis

Philip Melanchthon, author of the Augsburg Confession.

The Torgau Articles

In 1530, for the first time in nine years, Emperor Charles V was free to visit Germany. His wars with France were over for the time being, and he wanted very much to settle the religious problems that had kept Germany divided. The Turks were still threatening, and Charles needed all the help he could get to keep them away from his lands.

The emperor called for the diet to meet in Augsburg in late spring. He told the Lutheran princes to prepare a written statement of their beliefs and promised them a fair chance to present it.

Some of the Lutheran princes did not trust Charles, but Elector John of Saxony did. He asked Luther, Melanchthon, and Justus Jonas to write the statement for Charles. This statement of the Lutherans' beliefs was called the Torgau Articles because much of the writing was done in this Saxon town.

Luther was bitterly disappointed when Elector John would not let him travel to Augsburg. The elector realized that Luther was still an outlaw under the Edict of Worms, and he feared the reformer would not be safe outside of Saxony.

Much against his will, Luther agreed to remain at Coburg castle while his friends went on to Augsburg. At the Coburg, as at the Wartburg nine years earlier, Luther kept busy with Bible study and letter writing. For hours each day he prayed that God would take care of his friends and bring them success.

The Rewritten Torgau Articles—The Augsburg Confession

Meanwhile at Augsburg the enemies of Luther were telling Charles to use force to stamp out the new religion. Charles began to give in to them. He refused to allow Elector John to visit him and ordered the Protestants to stop preaching in Augsburg.

The emperor also had a copy of John Eck's latest book, which listed over four hundred "errors" in Luther's teachings. Eck had included many teachings of other reformers. He made it appear as if Luther taught all the heresies despised by the Roman Catholic Church. When Melanchthon read this book, he knew that the Torgau Articles would have to be rewritten and enlarged to answer Eck's false charges and to state clearly the scriptural teachings of the Lutherans.

Melanchthon worked hard and fast to write the new confession, not defense, of faith in time for the meetings at Augsburg. When he finished, he sent a copy to Luther, who was greatly pleased with it. This statement of faith, known as the Augsburg Confession, is one that Lutherans still today believe is a faithful statement of the teachings in God's Word.

In Augsburg the Lutheran princes bravely defended their faith. They refused to kneel before the pope's representative or at the special services in the cathedral. One prince even told the emperor to his face that he would let his head be cut off before he would forsake the Gospel of Jesus.

From the Augsburg Confession

IV. Concerning Justification

"We cannot obtain forgiveness of sin and righteousness before God through our merit, work, or satisfactions, but . . . we receive forgiveness of sin and become righteous before God out of grace for Christ's sake through faith." (AC IV 1–2)

VII. Concerning the Church

"At all times there must be and remain one holy, Christian church. It is the assembly of all believers among whom the gospel is purely preached and the holy sacraments are administered according to the gospel. For this is enough for the true unity of the Christian church that there the gospel is preached harmoniously according to a pure understanding and the sacraments are administered in conformity with the divine Word. It is not necessary for the true unity of the Christian church that uniform ceremonies, instituted by human beings, be observed everywhere." (AC VII 1–4)

X. Concerning the Lord's Supper

"The true body and blood of Christ are truly present under the form of bread and wine in the Lord's Supper and are distributed and received there." (AC X 1–2)

XXII. Concerning Both Kinds of the Sacrament

"Among us both kinds of the sacrament are given to the laity for the following reason. There is a clear order and command of Christ in Matthew 26[:27]: 'Drink from it, all of you.' Concerning the cup Christ here commands with clear words that they all should drink from it." (AC XXII 1–2)

XX. Concerning Faith and Good Works

"Good works should and must be done, not that a person relies on them to earn grace, but for God's sake and to God's praise. Faith alone always takes hold of grace and forgiveness of sin." (AC XX 27–29)

XXI. Concerning the Cult of the Saints

"Saints are to be remembered so that we may strengthen our faith when we see how they experienced grace and how they were helped by faith. Moreover, it is taught that each person, according to his or her calling, should take the saints' good works as an example. . . . However, it cannot be demonstrated from Scripture that a person should call upon the saints or seek help from them. 'For there is only one single reconciler and mediator set up between God and humanity, Jesus Christ' (1 Tim. 2[:5]). . . . He alone has promised to hear our prayers." (AC XXI 1–3)

Luther translated the Old Testament in 1534.

The Confession Is Read

On June 25, 1530, the emperor called the diet together in the bishop's palace. The room was completely filled with people, and many more stood in the halls and in the outside courtyard.

Dr. Christian Beyer, a court official of Saxony, stepped forward. He read the Augsburg Confession in German so loudly that even those outside could hear every word.

For two hours Dr. Beyer read. The Augsburg Confession (1530) stated what Lutherans believe about God, sin, faith, the Lord's Supper, Baptism, and many other doctrines. It quoted many passages from the Bible to show that these teachings were based on the Word of God. It clearly stated that the Lutherans did not teach the false teachings that Eck and others said they did. It also pointed out some teachings of the Roman church that were contrary to the Scriptures and showed how they had been corrected in the new churches. The Augsburg Confession tried to show that Luther's teachings were the same as those of the early Christians.

Five or six princes and the officers of two cities had signed the Confession. The leaders of five more free cities signed it after it was read, and more were to join them later. These people were risking their lives for the Gospel of Jesus Christ.

Some of the Catholic princes now heard for the first time what the Lutherans really believed. Many were surprised that their teachings were so scriptural. One of these princes asked John Eck if he could offer good arguments against the Lutherans. Eck replied that he could do so from the church fathers, but not from the Scriptures. "Are you telling me," the good Catholic duke then asked, "that the Lutherans are sitting inside the Scriptures while we are outside?"

The Emperor's Threat

Emperor Charles, however, was not convinced. He appointed men, led by Eck, to write a reply to the Augsburg Confession, pointing out its "errors." Very quickly this was done. When the emperor read it, however, he shook his head: "This will not do. You answer the Lutherans with scorn and hatred. Do it again, and this time use only the Bible in your arguments."

By August 3 another copy, called the Confutation, was ready; it was much shorter and was filled with Bible passages. The emperor then said he had read both the Lutheran and the Catholic statements, and he believed the Catholic one to be true and correct. When the Lutherans asked for a copy of the Confutation so they could prepare a reply, they were told they could not have a copy until they accepted it. There was no need for further debate. If they did not, they would feel "the edge of the sword."

The Lutheran princes would not give in. Elector John bravely stood up to the emperor and said he would suffer the loss of his life and lands before he would deny his Savior. The other princes, too, remained firm. God had truly answered Luther's prayers! The emperor gave those who had signed the Augsburg Confession until April 15, 1531, to decide if they would agree with the articles that had been presented by the Catholic princes.

Because the secretaries for the Lutheran princes took good notes on the reading of the Confutation, Melanchthon began preparing a defense of Lutheran beliefs in a paper called The Apology of the Augsburg Confession (1531). After several revisions, it was used along with the Augsburg Confession as a statement of Lutheran beliefs and today is included in the Book of Concord.

Six years later Luther and several colleagues prepared the Smalcald Articles (1537). This was Luther's own statement of what he believed and taught; it was also his list of what ought to be discussed if there ever was a papal council where Lutherans could participate.

God also kept His protecting arm over Luther's followers. Charles gave the Lutherans seven months to change their minds and return to the Roman church. During that time, however, new troubles arose that took all of Charles's attention. It was 15 years before he could again turn to German religious matters. During these years more and more people heard the Gospel preached in the Lutheran churches.

Because of pressure from the emperor and Catholic princes, the Lutherans were driven closer together. In February 1531 they formed the League of Schmalkalden. The day of reckoning never came because the emperor was too preoccupied with the problem of the Turks to deal with the Lutheran princes further. He signed the Peace of Nuremberg in July 1532. In this way the Reformation was allowed to proceed.

Review Questions and Study Projects

1. Underline the correct word or group of words in parentheses.

   a. Emperor Charles V wanted all Germans to unite to help fight the (Turks; English) in 1530.

   b. Luther had to stay at the (Wartburg; Coburg) while his friends went to the Diet of Augsburg.

   c. The Torgau Articles were rewritten because (they contained too many errors; Eck had accused the Lutherans of the false teachings of others).

   d. (Justus Jonas; Philip Melanchthon) wrote the Augsburg Confession.

   e. The Augsburg Confession was signed by (pastors and professors; princes and rulers).

   f. The Augsburg Confession showed that Luther's teachings were a return to those of (the early Christians; the Roman Catholic Church).

g. Many Catholics were surprised at the Augsburg Confession because (it was clearly based on God's Word; it was exactly like their own teachings).

h. Emperor Charles ordered the Lutherans (to give up their religious beliefs; to leave Germany and never return).

i. The emperor did not deal with the Lutherans of Germany for another 15 years because (they were too powerful for him; he had to tend to many other matters).

2. The Diet of Augsburg reminds us of several Bible stories in which children of God were true to their faith. Fill in the blanks in the following statements. Use your Bible to help you find answers.

a. At Augsburg Emperor _____ ordered the _____ to stop _____ and rejoin the Church of Rome.

b. Daniel 3:1–18: _____ the king ordered the _____ to fall down and _____ the golden image. _____, _____, and _____ refused to deny their faith in this way.

c. Daniel 6:1–10: _____ disobeyed the order of King _____, who said that no one should _____ to anyone but the king.

d. Acts 5:27–32: The _____ _____ commanded _____ to stop _____ about Jesus.

e. In all of these cases the orders of rulers were not obeyed. Study Acts 5:29 and explain why, in these cases, the action taken was in agreement with God's Word.

_____

_____

_____

_____

3. a. What is the Augsburg Confession?

_____

_____

_____

_____

b. Where did these teachings originate?

_____

_____

_____

_____

c. Why is the Augsburg Confession important for you?

_____

_____

_____

_____

4. a. How did God answer Luther's prayers for his friends in Augsburg?

_____

_____

_____

_____

b. Jesus prayed for His disciples (John 17:15). What was Jesus' prayer for His disciples? When the Holy Spirit prays for you (Romans 8:26), for what might He pray?

_____

_____

_____

_____

5. Define these terms: cathedral   duke

6. Map work: On the map on page 4 place a Q near Augsburg, an R near Torgau, and an S near the Coburg.

7. Write a paragraph telling how you can witness to the truth of God's Word in your life today and why it is important to do so.

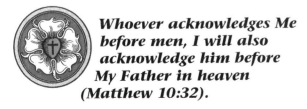
Whoever acknowledges Me before men, I will also acknowledge him before My Father in heaven (Matthew 10:32).

My Prayer

Dear Lord Jesus, give me the courage to confess You before others. Help me to tell others of Your love for them and the salvation they have in You. Guide me in all the things I do so that my life will honor You. In Your name I pray. Amen.

17 Luther, Servant to the End

Luther's Continuing Work

When the Lutheran theologians and princes left Augsburg, they all realized that there was much work left to do. They needed to fill Luther in on the details. They needed to revise and fine-tune the hastily written documents that had been used at Augsburg. They needed to ensure that the effort to reform the church so that the Gospel could be clearly taught and preached would continue.

While at the Coburg during the discussions at Augsburg, Luther had worked on explanations of the first 25 psalms. Psalm 118 was Luther's favorite psalm. When he could find no other help, "this psalm," he wrote, "proved a friend and helped me out of many great troubles."

In spite of a slowly healing leg injury, he also continued translating the Old Testament into German. In the sermons and writings he completed at the Coburg, he urged parents to keep their children in school, advocated more frequent participation in the Lord's Supper, and praised music as next to theology in importance in being able to bring peace and happiness to the soul.

His aide Veit Dietrich reported that Luther spent much time in prayer; it was evidence that his confident faith sprang from his deep devotion to God, which was nurtured by the Scriptures. He used his recently completed catechisms as guides for his prayers and meditations. All of these activities gave hints of what Luther would be doing in the years to come.

Luther and his party left Coburg castle on October 4, 1530, and returned to Wittenberg. In spite of ill health, he continued working to strengthen the churches. He was now sure that the Roman Catholic Church in which he had grown up could not be reformed. He was convinced that the evangelical churches that he worked with were the true church because they taught the Gospel clearly and administered the Sacraments as they had been instituted by God.

Strengthening the Church—The Postils

Years before Augsburg, Luther had begun writing materials to help pastors prepare sermons. These aids were called *postils*. In 1520 Frederick the Wise, who was impressed with Luther's preaching of the Gospel, had suggested that he prepare such materials. While at the Wartburg Luther completed his postils for the Christmas season, and they were printed in 1522. He had the postils for the Lenten season ready in 1525. One of Luther's students took notes on Luther's sermons and published them in 1526 and 1527 to provide ideas for pastors to use during the other parts of the church year. Several printers gathered these postils together and printed them in their own one-volume editions. Because of mistakes he found, Luther prepared editions of his postils throughout the 1530s and in 1540 and 1543. Each time he included the revisions he had made in his translation of the German Bible or ideas he was addressing at the time.

Pastors, some of whom had little training, scholars, and leaders of the new churches used the postils. Luther's scholarly explanations of Scripture and the sound doctrine that he taught helped many people understand that Jesus was the only way to salvation. Through them Luther planted the seeds of Lutheran teaching throughout Germany. Even now, his postils influence scriptural teaching throughout the world.

Strengthening the Church— The Catechisms

Luther had completed his catechisms in 1529, before the Diet of Augsburg. While visiting the churches in Saxony, he became convinced that pastors and teachers needed materials to help them understand and teach God's Word. Sermons that he preached in 1528 provided the basic content for the Large Catechism, which appeared in April 1529, and for the Small Catechism, which appeared one month later.

Teaching materials had been used in the early church for over a thousand years to prepare people for Baptism. The Creed, the Lord's Prayer, and the Ten Commandments were always included for study. Although many other topics had been added to the materials over the years, Luther chose to include these three and the Sacraments of Baptism and Holy Communion, together with Confession, in his catechisms. Because of his new understanding that salvation was by God's grace alone through faith alone, he omitted studying the Ave Maria and the other sacraments of the Roman Catholic Church.

His catechisms have been called "the Bible in miniature" because they helped pastors, teachers, and parents explain the teachings of Scripture. He advised that people be asked to answer questions from the catechism when they announced that they wanted to receive Holy Communion. In the years following the Diet of Augsburg, Luther continued to encourage pastors and teachers to study the catechism and to use it in their work. The pastors that he trained at the University of Wittenberg all had to study the catechism during their time of study.

Strengthening the Church— The German Bible

Following the Diet of Augsburg, Luther and his friends continued to translate the Old Testament into German. Soon after completing his translation of the New Testament in early 1522, he had begun work on the Old Testament. Since Luther was not a Hebrew scholar, he received help from Melanchthon, Amsdorf, and Aurogallus, the Hebrew professor at Wittenberg. Various parts of the Bible were printed as he finished them. At the Coburg he worked on the prophets Jeremiah

This woodcut of Jacob's ladder was included in Luther's Bible of 1534.

CPH

and Ezekiel. The complete German Bible was finally printed in 1534. Many woodcuts picturing Bible stories and beautifully illuminated initials were included in this edition.

This Bible quickly replaced the various Bibles being used in the churches at the time. The German translation made the people feel as if the characters in the Bible were talking to them in their everyday language. Luther's German Bible was used extensively in church services and in homes, and so it became Luther's crowning achievement.

Almost immediately after its printing, however, Luther began revising and improving it. He gathered together scholars to examine details and improve wording. He was determined that the German Bible carry God's message accurately. He conducted many meetings to check its accuracy; once he had several rams killed so that the local butcher could tell him the proper name for each part of the animal. The Wittenberg scholars who worked with him consulted Latin, Greek, and Hebrew texts. In 1531 16 scholars helped him revise the translation of the psalms. A revised German Bible was issued in September 1541. Other groups checked the accuracy of the work several times, the last time in 1544. In all of this work, Luther was a master both in leading the group and in knowing and using the various languages.

Strengthening the Church— The Liturgy and Hymns

During his school years Luther had shown that God had blessed him with musical skills. He was noted for his fine singing voice, and he loved to play the lute. As Luther came to understand that justification came by faith alone, he also realized that liturgies that taught that in the Sacrament Christ was sacrificed a second time had to be changed. As time went on, Luther gave greater importance to the sermon in the church service. He urged that German be used and encouraged the

singing of hymns by the congregation. Luther himself prepared new liturgies for the Communion service that were Christ-centered. All changes and additions to the service were made to emphasize the Gospel and bring praise to Christ. He avoided any unnecessary, abrupt changes that would upset the people.

To teach the doctrines of the church, to provide hymns for part of the liturgical service, and to make possible the use of the language of the people in church services, he composed several hymns, including "A Mighty Fortress Is Our God," "We All Believe in One True God," and the Communion hymn "O Lord, We Praise You." With Conrad Rupff and Johann Walther, the court musicians, he revised the Gregorian chants to fit the German texts. His *German Mass* was used in the Town Church in Wittenberg for the first time on Christmas Day 1525.

Luther's changes and his own hymn writing encouraged others to compose music and hymn texts and to produce hymnals. In a time when other Protestant leaders were destroying pipe organs and banning singing in the churches, Luther encouraged the use of music to teach the Gospel and enable the people to praise God. Due to his influence, Lutheran churches had hymns for all seasons and festivals of the church year by 1545. His use of music has inspired many church musicians to revise and compose music that proclaims the Gospel and teaches, while enabling the people to participate in worship through song.

Luther's Own Statement of Faith—The Smalcald Articles

Following the collapse of negotiations to have the Lutheran princes accept the Roman Catholic position at Augsburg, Germany became more divided. In November 1530 the Emperor declared that the church property of the Lutherans should be returned to the Roman Catholic Church. He also renewed the Edict of Worms, which declared that Luther was an outlaw. In response, in February 1531 the Lutheran princes formed the League of Schmalkalden to defend themselves.

In an effort to unite the Zwinglians and the Lutherans, Martin Bucer and Wolfgang Capito, theologians who had been associated with Zwingli, met with Luther and other Lutheran theologians to discuss their differences. After lengthy discussions about the Lord's Supper that were spread over several years, the two sides agreed that many of their differences had been resolved, and they signed the Wittenberg Concord in May 1536. However, differences concerning the Lord's Supper remain to this day.

During these years Luther decided that he would write his own statement of faith so that everyone would be clear about what Lutherans believed and taught. Not feeling well and thinking he would die soon, he did not want people to argue about his teachings when he was gone. He also thought his statement of faith would help unify the Lutherans when they met with papal representatives at the general Christian council called by the emperor to settle the problems of reform. When the pope called for a church council to meet in Mantua, Luther, in consultation with several of his associates, wrote his statements after Christmas 1536 and completed the Smalcald Articles in early January 1537.

Unfortunately, Luther became very ill and could not attend the meetings where they were to be presented. When Philip of Hesse criticized the statements, Melanchthon agreed to write other documents that were accepted. When Luther found out what happened, he carefully edited his own statements in the spring of 1538, and these Smalcald Articles began to be used alongside the Augsburg Confession and the Apology of the Augsburg Confession as statements of Lutheran teaching. They were a declaration of independence from the Roman Catholic Church.

> *Here is the first and chief article: That Jesus Christ, our God and Lord, "was handed over to death for our trespasses and was raised for our justification" (Romans 4[:25]); and he alone is "the Lamb of God, who takes away the sin of the world" (John 1[:29]); and "the Lord has laid on him the iniquity of us all" (Isa. 53[:6]); furthermore, "All have sinned," and "they are now justified without merit by his grace, through the redemption that is in Christ Jesus . . . by his blood" (Rom. 3[:23–25]).*
>
> *Now because this must be believed and may not be obtained or grasped otherwise with any work, law, or merit, it is clear and certain that this faith alone justifies us. (SA II 1–4)*

Luther's Difficulties

While Luther strengthened the churches in a variety of ways during the years after the Diet of Augsburg, he also faced many difficulties. He gave some embarrassingly bad advice to his supporter, Philip of Hesse, suggesting that Philip, who was already married, might also marry a second woman.

Luther referred to the marriages of some Old Testament patriarchs and assumed that the advice he gave would be kept secret because it was given during a confessional.

Luther's request that his advice be kept secret was impossible to keep. His advice that Philip could enter a bigamous marriage is in disagreement with the biblical teaching of 1 Timothy 3:2. For Luther, the whole episode was a disaster.

During these years Luther also made several unfortunate statements regarding

Pictured here is a reconstruction of the room in Eisleben in which Luther died in 1546.

the Jewish people and the papacy. In 1523 Luther had written that he hoped the Jews would be converted now that the Gospel was being taught clearly in the churches of the Reformation. When Elector John Frederick banished all Jews from his territories in 1536 and forbade them to travel through the territories, one of Europe's Hebrew scholars asked Luther to plead with the elector to allow Josel Rosheim, a Jewish leader of Hebrew scholars, to travel there. Luther refused. Disappointed at the Jews for not embracing the clear Gospel message, Luther regarded them as people who opposed Jesus and His saving grace. For twenty-first-century people who have seen the Holocaust, his statements about Jewish people are reprehensible. Those who do not know that Jesus is the Savior need to hear the Gospel, not be treated disdainfully.

His attacks on the papacy were equally vicious. He spoke of Pope Paul III as being "the Antichrist." In his tract *Against the Papacy of Rome, Founded by the Devil* (1545), he depicted the pope as being instructed by the devil. Some of Luther's writings, even while he was contending for the Gospel, bring him no honor.

Luther's Last Days and Death

For the rest of his life Luther continued to preach and teach in Wittenberg. His busy pen turned out many books, pamphlets, and letters. The Luther house was always open to visitors, and Katie and the children made the home a happy place for Dr. Luther.

But Luther's health began to fail. As a monk he had fasted much and slept little. As a reformer he never stopped working—preaching, teaching, and writing. Even a strong body could not stand such a load indefinitely.

In January 1546 he was called to Eisleben to settle a quarrel between two noblemen. The hard, cold trip brought Luther his final illness. On his deathbed the great reformer recited Scripture passages and asked God to receive his soul. Justus Jonas leaned over and asked, "Are you willing to die in the name of the Christ and the doctrine you have preached?"

Luther used his last remaining strength to answer clearly, "Yes."

It was his last word. In the very town where he had been born over 62 years earlier, he fell asleep in Jesus on the morning of February 18, 1546, surrounded by friends and two of his sons.

In spite of his faults, Luther was, by God's grace, a religious genius, a man of courage, and a person devoted to the clear teaching of the Gospel. Where the Christian faith was concerned, he would not compromise. A word of Scripture that might well be applied to this servant of God is this passage: "Well done, good and faithful servant!" (Matthew 25:21).

Review Questions and Study Projects

1. If the statement is true, circle the T. If it is false, circle the F.

T   F   a. The changes Luther worked to bring to the churches involved making sure the churches taught the Gospel clearly.

T   F   b. Postils are intended to help rulers write laws that improve the church.

T   F   c. The main parts of the catechisms are the Ten Commandments and the Ave Maria.

T   F   d. Luther consulted many people as he translated the Old Testament into German.

T   F   e. Luther did not want the liturgy of the church to be changed at all.

T   F   f. The confession of the Lutheran church written by Luther is the Augsburg Confession.

T   F   g. Luther advised Philip of Hesse to take a second wife.

T   F   h. Luther died in the same town in which he was born.

2. Why would Luther's catechisms be called "the Bible in miniature"?

_____

_____

_____

3. What would Luther look for in a song that was being considered for use in a worship service?

_____

_____

_____

4. Why did Luther write the Smalcald Articles?

_____

_____

_____

5. Since Luther was concerned about the Gospel, why do Lutherans and others who are living now condemn some of his statements about Catholics and Jewish people?

_____

_____

_____

6. Describe how you might use Luther's Small Catechism as a guide for your own prayers.

_____

_____

_____

7. What are the great contributions that Luther made to the church and people everywhere?

_____

_____

_____

8. On the map on page 4 place a + near the town in which Luther was born and also died.

_____

_____

_____

9. Define these words:

chant_____

justification_____

bigamous _____

10. Prepare a presentation on one of these topics:

The thoughts in one of Luther's hymns
Justus Jonas
Martin Bucer
Johann Bugenhagen
The Book of Concord

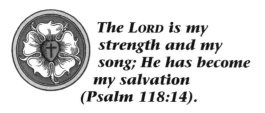

The LORD is my strength and my song; He has become my salvation (Psalm 118:14).

My Prayer

O Lord God, heavenly Father, pour out Your Holy Spirit on Your faithful people, keep them steadfast in Your grace and truth, protect and comfort them in all temptation, defend them against all enemies of Your Word, and bestow on Christ's Church Militant Your saving peace; through Jesus Christ, Your Son, our Lord, who lives and reigns with You and the Holy Spirit, one God, now and forever. Amen.

From the Collect for Commemoration of the Doctors of the Church, *Lutheran Worship*, p. 110.

CPSIA information can be obtained at www.ICGtesting.com
Printed in the USA
LVOW011453111012

302457LV00001B/2/P